W9-CDB-116

Cooking with
Beyond® and
Impossible™ Meat

Cooking with
Beyond® and Impossible™ Meat

60 Vegan Recipes Using Plant-Based Substitutions

Ramin Ganeshram
co-author of *The Art of the Perfect Sauce*

PAGE STREET
PUBLISHING CO.

PAGE STREET
PUBLISHING CO.

Copyright © 2021 Ramin Ganeshram

First published in 2021 by
Page Street Publishing Co.
27 Congress Street, Suite 105
Salem, MA 01970
www.pagestreetpublishing.com

All rights reserved. No part of this book may be reproduced or used, in any form or by any means, electronic or mechanical, without prior permission in writing from the publisher.

Distributed by Macmillan, sales in Canada by The Canadian Manda Group.

25   24   23   22   21   1   2   3   4   5

ISBN-13: 978-1-64567-251-7
ISBN-10: 1-64567-251-4

Library of Congress Control Number: 2020944081

Cover and book design by Kylie Alexander for Page Street Publishing Co.
Photography by Toni Zernick
Food and prop styling by Toni Zernick

Printed and bound in the United States

Page Street Publishing protects our planet by donating to nonprofits like The Trustees, which focuses on local land conservation.

For Victoria

Table
of
Contents

Know Your Alternative Meats: A Primer

Close-to-the-real-thing alternative meats have been on the market longer than people may realize—notably in the form of textured soy protein bits. One example is the Betty Crocker™ brand Bac-Os "bacon bits" that have been on the shelves for decades and are a popular topping at many salad bars. While soy-based alternative meats graduated into burgers and hot dogs around the same time, they were notable for their strange texture—not like meat at all but certainly packing a protein punch. Textured vegetable protein and textured soy protein were stand-ins for ground meat that approximated texture but didn't fool meat lovers.

For a long time, these soy-based alternative meats comprised the majority of the market. In the 2000s, companies were looking to create alternatives when soy got a bad rap as an estrogen receptor that was potentially harmful for those at risk for breast cancer or breast cancer patients—a belief since debunked by scientists. Some of those alternatives—like Quorn™—use mushroom protein in place of soy, and others use a more processed form of legume.

Modern plant-based alternative meats are a far cry from early options—believably approximating animal meat in their look, smell and taste. More crucially, their texture is often indiscernible from their animal-based counterparts. This is important for creating dishes that will leave you both satisfied and wanting more. Happily, there is a large international canon of ground meat recipes—likely because ground meat is more economical than more expensive cuts—meaning there is a wonderful variety of dishes for which to use alternative meats.

The two major brands on the market—Impossible™ meat and Beyond Meat®—come in enough variety that it's easy to substitute them for meat in an array of dishes including appetizers, soups and sides, but the best news is for the main course. There are sausages, patties, ground "meat" options and crumbles. This may leave you asking: Which alternative meat should I choose? The answer lies in what you want to prepare and, as with any recipe, what flavor profile you're looking for. This book focuses on the following brands and options for both variety and availability on the market:

Beyond Meat®: The Beyond Meat® company started like Impossible™ Burger with a simple pre-formed hamburger you could make at home that smells like a beef burger and even "bleeds." The company has brought other options to market very quickly, including 1-pound (454-g) ground "meat" packages, crumbles, sausage patties and sausages. Taking into account the texture and taste of the product, this book has recipes for each. For example, while the 1-pound (454-g) packages of ground meat are great for kebabs because of their fat content, they're not as good for tacos—the crumbles are better suited for that. Also, look for the "raw" product to be used in recipes where we will want to break up the meat finely versus having larger crumbles. Beyond Meat® is the go-to for those who are also avoiding gluten and soy in their alternative meats.

Impossible™ meat: The other biggest player in the alternative meat market is Impossible Foods, which first hit the market in the fast-food world with the Impossible™ Burger—and is still a bestseller. Unlike, Beyond Meat®, Impossible Foods' raw "meat" product comes in a 12-ounce (340-g) versus 16-ounce (454-g) package. Still, you can generally use the Impossible Foods 12-ounce (340-g) package in recipes calling for 16 ounces or 1 pound (454 g) of "meat." This is because the shrinkage on the Impossible Foods brand of products is less than other alternative meats.

Like Beyond Meat®, Impossible™ meat products do not have gluten—although an early iteration of the brand did contain wheat protein—but they do have soy.

Impossible Foods has also created a sausage patty that, as of this writing, has yet to hit the supermarket aisles. The company is also perfecting an Impossible™ Pork product. If the quality of the beef-type product is any indication, the Impossible™ Sausage and Impossible™ Pork will prove a wonderful addition to the vegan meat repertoire for dishes that don't require the heavier, fattier taste of "beef"-type substitutes. See the list below for recipes for which you can substitute Impossible™ Pork when it hits the grocery store market:

Thai-Style Sweet Chili Meatballs (page 21)
Sesame-Ginger-Soy Meatballs (page 25)
Jerk-Seasoned Meatballs (page 27)
Chinese-Style Dumplings (page 80)
Shroom Lettuce Cups (page 83)
Thai-Style Red Curry Coconut Soup (page 87)
Szechuan-Style String Beans & Ground Meat (page 88)
Mee Krob (page 91)
Moo Shu (page 92)
Classic Italian Meatballs (page 107)
Classic Italian Tomato Meat Sauce (page 108)

Trader Joe's® and Other Store Brands: Where possible, this book will offer options such as the Trader Joe's® store brand of meatless burgers, meat and Turkeyless turkey burgers, or protein patties as they are branded. I have found, however, that while many of them are very good, they are not quite on par with the branded products listed on the previous page.

Tips & Techniques

Frozen vs. Raw

Unlike real ground meat, many of these products do not do well when prepared from a purely frozen state. "Raw meat" alternatives do not retain their shape and texture when cooked from frozen. Most "crumble" products are, however, meant to be cooked while frozen and will maintain their quality.

Defrosting & Storage

Both Impossible™ meat and Beyond Meat® products should be defrosted in the refrigerator until completely soft. Store either for up to ten days in the refrigerator and do not refreeze.

Additionally, throughout the book you'll find tips and techniques to use these products to their best advantage in specific recipes, as well as advice regarding which is best suited to your recipe because not all alternative meats are alike. Also included are tips on freezing raw and cooked preparations and making ahead, as well as what cooking preparations really work—and what preparations don't. For example, burgers and kebabs really don't do well straight on the barbecue grill, but they can be started on a sheet of tinfoil and then moved directly onto the grill later.

Impossible Foods and Beyond Meat® alternatives are constantly expanding their lines of products with a wide range that include a variety of textures from "raw meat" to crumbles and sausage, which are more suited for dishes beyond entrées. You'll find a variety of recipes for every meal occasion—from appetizers, soups and small bites that are perfect for a party or as the beginning of a meal for a crowd.

But the main course is where alternative meats really shine, and they are excellent for making vegan meals heartier and more filling. Don't discount the fact that these "meaty" substitutes can also be used for lighter fare like kebabs and stir-fries.

With recipes from around the world that originally use ground meats as their base, there's a good variety of dishes in this book for all tastes and texture lovers. You'll find that the book is organized by flavor profile to help you feed your yen for a particular craving quickly. The book is also entirely vegan, although lacto-vegetarians will find it easy to substitute the "real" thing when sour cream, yogurt or cheese are called for in recipes—but modern vegan alternatives are so good, you won't have to.

CHAPTER 1

All-American Faves

Classic Chili

2 tsp (10 ml) safflower oil

1 small onion, chopped small

2 to 3 cloves garlic, minced

1 package Beyond Meat® or Impossible™ meat

1 tsp chili powder or more to taste

1 tsp unsweetened cocoa powder

2 tbsp (32 g) tomato paste

1 (15-oz [425-g]) can diced fire-roasted tomatoes

2 cups (480 ml) vegetable stock

1 (15-oz [425-g]) can black beans, drained and rinsed

1 (15-oz [425-g]) can dark red kidney beans, drained and rinsed

1 tsp coarse salt

Chopped fresh cilantro, for garnish (optional)

1 cup (113 g) shredded vegan cheddar cheese, for garnish (optional)

½ cup (120 ml) vegan sour cream or toum (Middle Eastern garlic dip), for garnish (optional)

Cornbread, for serving (optional)

Unsweetened cocoa powder gives this classic chili an extra "meaty" flavor. This bean-rich chili is perfect with cornbread for a full-on hearty meal. The recipe calls for canned or boxed beans, but reconstituted dried beans work very well too. Just make sure they are thoroughly cooked before adding since this chili does not have the long cooking time that animal-protein versions do. See below for how to reconstitute dried beans. Sour cream is a popular topping for chili and there are some good vegan versions on the market, but I also find that Middle Eastern–style garlic topping (toum), which is simply whipped garlic and oil, has a lovely texture and flavor.

Heat a large, wide-mouth saucepan over medium heat and add the safflower oil. Add the onion and fry for 6 to 7 minutes, or until it begins to soften and become translucent, and add the garlic. Fry for 1 minute more.

Add the alternative meat and break it up with a wooden spoon into small pieces. Fry until lightly browned, 5 to 6 minutes.

Stir in the chili powder and unsweetened cocoa powder and mix well. Fry for 1 minute and add the tomato paste, stirring well. Fry for 1 minute more.

Add the tomatoes and vegetable stock and stir very well. Reduce the heat to a simmer.

Stir in the drained beans and salt and mix well. Simmer until the liquid is reduced by two-thirds, 10 to 12 minutes.

Serve hot garnished with cilantro, if desired. Serve with cheese, sour cream and cornbread, if desired.

Using Dried Beans

Dried beans are economical and versatile because you can control the consistency, whereas many canned or boxed versions can wind up too mushy for some recipes. The rule of thumb for reconstituting and cooking any dried bean is 3 cups (720 ml) of water to 1 cup (184 g) of beans. Here's how you do it: Soak the beans overnight, drain them and then cook using the same ratio of water to beans. Don't add salt to your beans when cooking—it will make them tough. To speed along the process, you can add a pinch of baking soda. Pressure cookers are excellent for beans as well. I like to drain cooked beans and then store them in zip-top bags in the freezer (make sure to squeeze all the air out) so they are ready to use when I want them.

Serves 4

Beef & Barley Soup

½ cup (100 g) barley

1½ tsp (9 g) salt, divided

2 tsp (10 ml) olive oil

1 carrot, peeled, trimmed and chopped small

1 rib celery, trimmed and chopped small

½ small onion, minced

2 cloves garlic, minced

1 cup (70 g) chopped mushrooms

1 package Beyond Beef® Crumbles

1 tsp paprika

½ tsp minced thyme leaves

1 cup (60 g) chopped parsley

½ tsp freshly ground black pepper

1 bay leaf

1 quart (960 ml) vegetable stock

1 cup (180 g) chopped tomatoes

For chilly winter days, this hearty soup is perfect paired with a crusty loaf of bread. Barley is a filling grain that is high in fiber—it is not, however, gluten-free. Those seeking a gluten-free substitute should consider Chinese pearl barley, also known as "Job's tears." Simply cook according to package directions and substitute for traditional barley in this recipe.

Cook the barley: Add the barley, ½ teaspoon of the salt and 2 cups (480 ml) of water to a saucepan over medium heat and bring to a simmer. Cook the barley for 40 minutes. It will still be al dente and not cooked all the way through.

Make the soup: Heat the olive oil in a medium to large saucepan over medium heat and add the carrot and celery. Fry for 2 to 3 minutes and then add the onion. Fry for 6 to 7 minutes, or until the onion begins to soften and become translucent, then add the garlic and cook for 1 minute.

Stir in the mushrooms and fry for 2 to 3 minutes before adding the alternative meat. Fry the crumbles for 6 to 7 minutes then add the paprika, thyme leaves and parsley and mix well.

Stir in the remaining salt and pepper and cook for 1 minute. Add the bay leaf, vegetable stock and tomatoes and stir very well. Stir in the parcooked barley and reduce heat to a simmer. Cook, partially covered, for 20 minutes.

Make sure to remove the bay leaf before serving. Serve hot with crusty bread.

Bacon Cheeseburger Sliders

1 tbsp (14 g) vegan butter

1 small onion, thinly sliced

¼ cup (28 g) Betty Crocker™ Bac-Os or other vegan bacon bits

1 cup (113 g) shredded vegan cheddar cheese

¼ cup (14 g) plus 1 tbsp (4 g) sun-dried tomatoes, divided

1 package Beyond Meat® or Impossible™ meat

1 tsp garlic powder

½ tsp paprika

¼ tsp celery salt

½ tsp salt

¼ tsp freshly ground black pepper

2 tsp (10 ml) safflower oil

Rolls, for serving

Shredded lettuce, for garnish (optional)

In this recipe, vegan bacon bits, cheddar cheese and caramelized onion pack a flavor punch to create over-the-top mini burgers. Small dinner rolls are excellent to use as slider buns. These are great to round out an appetizer buffet or perfect for a meal to serve four.

Add the butter to a large frying pan over medium heat. When the butter melts, add the onion and reduce the heat to medium-low. Fry until the onion is browned and caramelized, 8 to 10 minutes. Remove from the pan and set aside in a small bowl.

In a large bowl, combine the Bac-Os, cheese, tomatoes, alternative meat, garlic powder, paprika, celery salt, salt and pepper. Mix well using your hands, then form into 12 equal-sized balls.

Flatten each ball into a small patty about ½ inch (1.3 cm) thick. Reheat the large frying pan in which you cooked the onion over medium heat and add the safflower oil. Add the burgers to the pan, leaving about 2 inches (5 cm) of space between each. Do not crowd the burgers in the pan. Fry in batches if needed.

Fry the burgers for 3 to 4 minutes on each side, or until lightly seared. Remove from the pan.

Alternatively, you may place all the patties on a sheet tray and bake at 350°F (177°C) for 10 to 12 minutes.

Place each patty on a small roll with an equal amount of caramelized onion. Add shredded lettuce, if desired.

Serve warm.

Mini Meatballs Five Ways

Mini meatballs are popular for parties or a fun finger-food-type meal. They're also versatile because they can be used as an appetizer when speared with a toothpick with dipping sauce on the side, yet they can be just as easily used as an entrée with pasta, a side vegetable or even in a soup. Each of these recipes feature a multiethnic twist that will liven up your spread.

While most of the recipes call for frying the meatballs, they can be baked too. Bake meatballs in a 350°F (177°C) oven for 15 minutes. Each mini meatball recipe serves four as an entrée or up to eight as an appetizer. Put together a variety for a full party platter and your guests will be delighted!

Thai-Style Sweet Chili Meatballs

Makes 24 meatballs

2 (8-oz [227-g]) packages Trader Joe's® Turkeyless Protein Patties

4 cloves garlic, grated

2 scallions, minced

1 tsp soy sauce

2 tsp (10 ml) fresh lime juice

½ tsp salt

½ tsp freshly ground black pepper

¼ cup (60 ml) safflower oil, for frying

1 cup (240 ml) Thai-style sweet chili sauce

Thai-style sweet chili sauce is the glaze for these mini meatballs flavored with garlic, ginger, basil and lemon zest. These are excellent as an addition to a Thai-style veggie soup that you can make by adding the meatballs to vegetable broth seasoned with garlic, ginger and coconut milk.

Make the meatballs: Combine all the ingredients except the safflower oil and sweet chili sauce in a large bowl and knead well with your hands until completely combined. Form into 24 equal-sized balls—roughly the size of a walnut.

Heat a large frying pan over medium heat and add the oil. Heat the oil for 3 to 4 minutes and add the meatballs in a single layer. Do not crowd the pan—fry the meatballs in batches if necessary. Fry for 3 to 4 minutes and then turn them over and fry the other side. Remove the meatballs with a slotted spoon and set aside.

Drain all the oil from the pan, then add the sweet chili sauce and the meatballs to the pan. Toss well to coat. Serve hot.

Swedish Meatballs

Swedish meatballs are a fun fan favorite. You can serve these as an appetizer or over wide noodles such as pappardelle for a full-size meal.

Make the meatballs: Combine all the ingredients except the safflower oil in a large bowl and knead well with your hands until completely combined. Form into 24 equal-sized balls—roughly the size of a walnut.

Heat a large frying pan over medium heat and add the oil. Heat the oil for 3 to 4 minutes and add the meatballs in a single layer. Do not crowd the pan—fry the meatballs in batches if necessary. Fry for 3 to 4 minutes and then turn them over and fry the other side. Remove the meatballs with a slotted spoon and set aside.

Make the sauce: Drain all but 1 tablespoon (15 ml) of oil from the frying pan and add the butter. When the butter melts, add the flour and, using a whisk, mix well for 1 to 2 minutes. The mixture will bubble and begin to look light brown.

Add the vegetable stock slowly, whisking the entire time in order to prevent lumps. Stir in the cream and whisk very well.

Add the onion powder, salt, pepper and the thyme sprig. Stir in the marsala wine, if using. Reduce heat to a simmer and cook for 4 to 5 minutes, or until the mixture begins to thicken.

Return the meatballs to the pan and simmer for 3 to 4 minutes, uncovered. Add the fresh parsley and serve.

For the meatballs

1 package Beyond Meat® or Impossible™ meat

½ onion, grated

4 cloves garlic, grated

½ tsp salt

½ tsp freshly ground black pepper

⅛ tsp nutmeg

2 tsp (10 ml) Worcestershire sauce

¼ cup (27 g) regular or gluten-free breadcrumbs

2 tbsp (3 g) dried parsley

¼ cup (60 ml) liquid egg substitute

¼ cup (60 ml) safflower oil, for frying

For the sauce

3 tbsp (42 g) vegan butter such as Earth Balance®

2 tbsp (16 g) flour or gluten-free flour

2 cups (480 ml) vegetable stock

1 pint (480 ml) dairy-free heavy cream

½ tsp onion powder

½ tsp salt

Freshly ground black pepper to taste

1 sprig fresh thyme

1 tsp marsala wine (optional)

¼ cup (15 g) minced fresh parsley

Brown Sugar Chili Meatballs

For the meatballs

1 package Beyond Meat® or Impossible™ meat

½ onion, grated

4 cloves garlic, grated

¼ tsp cayenne pepper

1 tbsp (14 g) dark brown sugar

½ tsp salt

½ tsp freshly ground black pepper

¼ cup (27 g) regular or gluten-free breadcrumbs

¼ cup (60 ml) liquid egg substitute

¼ cup (60 ml) safflower oil, for frying

For the sauce

3 tbsp (18 g) minced onion

1 tsp minced garlic

2 tbsp (28 g) dark brown sugar

1 tbsp (16 g) tomato paste

¼ cup (60 ml) plain tomato sauce

2 tsp (10 ml) Worcestershire sauce

1 cup (240 ml) vegetable stock

½ tsp onion powder

¼ tsp celery salt

½ tsp coarse salt

Freshly ground black pepper to taste

1 sprig fresh thyme

1 tsp bourbon (optional)

These little meatballs pack a sweet and spicy punch that's intensified by barbecue sauce with a similar flavor profile as a dipping sauce or glaze.

Make the meatballs: Combine all the ingredients except the safflower oil in a large bowl and knead well with your hands until completely combined. Form into 24 equal-sized balls—roughly the size of a walnut.

Heat a large frying pan over medium heat and add the oil. Heat the oil for 3 to 4 minutes and add the meatballs in a single layer. Do not crowd the pan—fry the meatballs in batches if necessary. Fry for 3 to 4 minutes and then turn them over and fry the other side. Remove the meatballs with a slotted spoon and set aside.

Make the sauce: Drain all but 2 tablespoons (30 ml) of oil from the frying pan and add the onion and garlic. Fry for 2 to 3 minutes. Add the brown sugar and cook, stirring until the sugar melts and begins to bubble.

Stir in the tomato paste and cook, stirring for about 1 minute. Add the tomato sauce and mix well. Stir in the Worcestershire sauce and then add the vegetable stock. You may use a whisk to prevent lumps from forming.

Add the onion powder, celery salt, salt, pepper and the thyme sprig. Stir in the bourbon, if using. Reduce heat to a simmer and cook for 6 to 7 minutes, or until the mixture begins to thicken.

Return the meatballs to the pan and simmer for 2 to 3 minutes, uncovered. Serve hot.

Sesame-Ginger-Soy Meatballs

For the meatballs

2 (8-oz [226-g]) packages Trader Joe's® Turkeyless Protein Patties

2 cloves garlic, grated

2 tsp (10 g) grated ginger

2 scallions, minced

1 tsp soy sauce

½ tsp toasted sesame oil

½ tsp salt

½ tsp freshly ground black pepper

¼ cup (60 ml) safflower oil, for frying

For the sauce

1 shallot, minced

1 clove garlic, minced

1 tsp ginger, minced

¼ cup (60 ml) mirin

¼ cup (60 ml) soy sauce

1 tsp dark brown sugar

2 cups (480 ml) vegetable stock

1 tsp cornstarch dissolved in 2 tsp (10 ml) hot water

Sesame seeds, for garnish

This savory, aromatic meatball is nice as part of a dim sum platter with accompaniments like sautéed bok choy, dumplings (page 80) and fried wontons (page 84).

Make the meatballs: Combine all the ingredients except the safflower oil in a large bowl and knead well with your hands until completely combined. Form into 24 equal-sized balls—roughly the size of a walnut.

Heat a large frying pan over medium heat and add the oil. Heat the oil for 3 to 4 minutes and add the meatballs in a single layer. Do not crowd the pan—fry the meatballs in batches if necessary. Fry for 3 to 4 minutes and then turn them over and fry the other side. Remove the meatballs with a slotted spoon and set aside.

Make the sauce: Drain all but 1 tablespoon (15 ml) of oil from the pan and add the shallot, garlic and ginger and stir well. Fry for 1 to 2 minutes. Add the mirin, soy sauce, brown sugar and vegetable stock and mix well. Reduce heat to a simmer and cook for 3 minutes. Stir in the cornstarch mixture and mix well.

Return the meatballs to the pan and simmer for an additional 4 to 5 minutes. Toss well to coat.

Serve hot garnished with sesame seeds.

Makes 24 meatballs

Jerk-Seasoned Meatballs

For the meatballs

1 package Impossible™ meat

½ onion, grated

4 cloves garlic, grated

¼ tsp cayenne pepper

1 tbsp (14 g) dark brown sugar

½ tsp salt

½ tsp freshly ground black pepper

¼ cup (27 g) regular or gluten-free
breadcrumbs

¼ cup (60 ml) liquid egg substitute

¼ cup (60 ml) safflower oil,
for frying

For the sauce:

3 tbsp (18 g) minced onion

1 tsp minced garlic

2 tbsp (28 g) dark brown sugar

1 tbsp (16 g) tomato paste

¼ cup (60 ml) plain tomato sauce

2 tsp (12 g) jerk seasoning

1 cup (240 ml) vegetable stock

½ tsp onion powder

¼ tsp celery salt

½ tsp coarse salt

Freshly ground black pepper to taste

1 sprig fresh thyme

1 tsp rum (optional)

I like to use Impossible™ meat for this recipe because it has a lighter taste and a texture that more closely approximates pork—the most traditional jerked meat. This recipe calls specifically for wet jerk seasoning and I prefer the Walkerswood brand, which is the most authentic one on the market.

Make the meatballs: Combine all the ingredients except the safflower oil in a large bowl and knead well with your hands until completely combined. Form into 24 equal-sized balls—roughly the size of a walnut.

Heat a large frying pan over medium heat and add the oil. Heat the oil for 3 to 4 minutes and add the meatballs in a single layer. Do not crowd the pan—fry the meatballs in batches if necessary. Fry for 3 to 4 minutes and then turn them over and fry the other side. Remove the meatballs with a slotted spoon and set aside.

Make the sauce: Drain all but 2 tablespoons (30 ml) of oil from the frying pan and add the onion and garlic. Fry for 2 to 3 minutes. Add the dark brown sugar and cook, stirring until the sugar melts and begins to bubble.

Stir in the tomato paste and cook, stirring for about 1 minute. Add the tomato sauce and mix well. Stir in the jerk seasoning and then add the vegetable stock. Add the onion powder, celery salt, salt, pepper, thyme sprig and rum, if using. Reduce heat to a simmer and cook for 4 to 5 minutes, or until the mixture begins to slightly thicken.

Return the meatballs to the pan and simmer for 3 to 4 minutes, uncovered. Serve hot.

More-than-a-Melt Patty Melt

2 tbsp (30 ml) safflower oil

1 large sweet onion, thinly sliced

1 package Beyond Meat® or Impossible™ meat

1 tsp onion powder

1 tsp garlic powder

½ tsp paprika

½ tsp celery salt

¼ tsp freshly ground black pepper

1 tbsp (15 ml) Worcestershire sauce

8 pats Earth Balance® or other vegan butter

8 slices rye bread or bread of your choice

4 slices vegan provolone cheese

Patty melts are a cross between a cheeseburger, a panini and a Philly cheesesteak. Made with an oblong patty, pressed thinner than a traditional burger, the patty melt features cheese and caramelized onion and is pressed down with a heavy weight in a frying pan. You can assemble the sandwiches and keep them in the refrigerator for up to one day before frying.

Make the caramelized onion: Heat the safflower oil in a large frying pan over medium heat and add the onion. Lower the heat to medium-low and cook the onion slowly, until softened and deep golden brown, about 20 minutes. Scrape the onion into a bowl and set aside. Reserve the pan.

Make the patties: Combine the alternative meat, onion and garlic powders, paprika, celery salt, pepper and Worcestershire sauce in a large bowl and knead to mix well. Form the mixture into four equal-sized portions and form these into oblong patties that match the size of your bread.

Heat the same pan in which you cooked the onion over medium heat. When the pan is hot, add the patties and cook, 4 minutes on each side. Remove from the pan.

Assemble the sandwiches: Have a large piece of parchment or waxed paper ready. Spread the butter on one side of each slice of bread. Place 4 of the slices, butter side down, on the parchment paper and place a cooked patty on top. Divide the caramelized onion into four equal portions and place one portion on top of the patty, and layer the cheese on top. Put another slice of bread, unbuttered side down, on top of the cheese. Repeat with all the patties, bread, cheese and caramelized onion.

Cook the patty melts: Heat a clean frying pan over medium heat and add the sandwiches (buttered side should be down). Don't crowd them in the pan—cook in batches if necessary.

Cook the sandwiches for 2 to 3 minutes, then turn them over. Use a sandwich press or a flat pan lid on top of which you can place cans of soup, vegetables or other weights to press down on each sandwich. Cook this way for 2 minutes more. Serve hot.

Superstar Salisbury Steak

1 package Beyond Meat® or Impossible™ meat

1 tsp onion powder

1 tsp garlic powder

½ tsp paprika

½ tsp celery salt

¼ tsp freshly ground black pepper

¼ cup (60 ml) vegan liquid egg substitute

¼ cup (27 g) regular or gluten-free breadcrumbs

2 tbsp (28 g) Earth Balance® or other vegan butter

1 small onion, minced

1 cup (230 g) sliced cremini mushrooms

2 tsp (10 g) tomato paste

1 tbsp (8 g) flour

1 cup (240 ml) vegetable stock

1 tbsp (15 ml) Worcestershire sauce

½ tsp salt

½ cup (120 ml) vegan heavy cream

¼ tsp thyme leaves

Like a lot of people, my first intro to Salisbury steak was in a frozen TV dinner or as the "mystery meat" in the school cafeteria. Neither of these did justice to what is actually a delicious dish, which features a creamy sauce that's perfect with mashed potatoes, egg noodles or even rice.

Make the steaks: Combine the alternative meat, onion and garlic powders, paprika, celery salt, pepper, egg and breadcrumbs in a large bowl and knead to mix well. Form the mixture into four equal-sized portions and form these into oblong patties that are about 5 inches (13 cm) long and 2½ inches (6 cm) wide.

Heat a large frying pan over medium heat and spray with baking spray or brush with olive oil. When the pan is hot, add the steaks and cook, 4 minutes on each side. Remove from the pan and set aside.

Melt the butter in the same frying pan that you cooked the steaks in and then add the onion. Cook for 6 to 7 minutes, or until the onion is translucent and has softened. Add the mushrooms and stir well. Cook for 7 minutes more. Add the tomato paste and stir well, cooking for 1 minute. Add the flour and cook for 2 minutes more.

Stir in the vegetable stock slowly, mixing the whole time to ensure there are no lumps of flour. Add the Worcestershire sauce and salt and simmer for 5 minutes. Add the cream and thyme leaves and simmer for 7 to 8 minutes more, or until thickened enough to coat a spoon. Add the steak patties back to the pan and simmer for 1 to 2 minutes. Serve hot.

Sloppy Joes

2 tsp (10 ml) safflower oil

1 small onion, minced

1 small green bell pepper, minced

3 cloves garlic, minced

1 package Beyond Meat® or Impossible™ meat

1 tbsp (16 g) tomato paste

½ cup (120 ml) ketchup

1 tsp yellow mustard

1 tbsp (14 g) dark brown sugar

1 tsp salt

½ tsp black pepper

¼ tsp cayenne pepper

½ tsp paprika

Buns or rolls, for serving

I often think of Sloppy Joes as deconstructed meatloaf that can be heaped upon a hamburger bun. Plump brioche-type buns are very nice for this because of their doughy texture. Serve Sloppy Joes with a side of French fries, yucca fries or potato chips.

Heat the safflower oil in a large frying pan over medium heat. Add the onion and bell pepper and fry for 6 to 7 minutes, or until the onion begins to soften and become translucent. Stir in the garlic and fry for 1 minute more.

Add the alternative meat and break up with a wooden spoon. Fry until browned, 6 to 7 minutes.

Add the tomato paste and stir very well, cooking for about 2 minutes. Stir in the ketchup, mustard, brown sugar, salt, pepper, cayenne pepper and paprika. Add 1 cup (240 ml) of water and mix very well.

Reduce heat to a simmer and cook until the water is reduced by two-thirds, 8 to 10 minutes. Serve in equal portions on burger buns or soft rolls.

American Chop Suey

2 tsp (10 ml) safflower oil

1 small onion, minced

½ green bell pepper, minced

3 cloves garlic, minced

1 package Beyond Meat® or Impossible™ meat

½ tsp dried oregano

1 tsp salt

½ tsp freshly ground black pepper

1 cup (180 g) canned diced tomatoes

1 cup (240 ml) tomato sauce

12 oz (340 g) cooked elbow macaroni (you may use gluten-free)

Grated vegan Parmesan cheese such as Violife, for serving (optional)

Legend has it that chop suey was created by West Coast Chinese restaurateurs in the beginning of the 20th century to appeal to the American palate. The dish was comprised of noodles, small pieces of meat and vegetables flavored with soy sauce. American chop suey, created in New England, was a cheap and filling meal so named because of the similar components to the Chinese American version: pasta, meat and vegetables. Thanks to tomato sauce and chopped tomatoes, American chop suey has a more Italian flair and is still a popular, casserole-type meal choice to feed a crowd.

Heat the safflower oil in a large frying pan over medium heat and add the onion and bell pepper. Cook for 5 to 6 minutes, or until the onion has softened and become translucent. Add the garlic and fry for 1 minute more.

Add the alternative meat and use a wooden spoon to break up the chunks. Cook until browned on all sides, 6 to 7 minutes.

Stir in the oregano, salt, pepper, tomatoes and tomato sauce and simmer for 2 to 3 minutes. Add the cooked macaroni to the pan and mix well.

Serve hot with Parmesan cheese, if desired.

Meatloaf Three Ways

Meatloaf is the classic American comfort food that can be prepared simply or in the most elevated form. These three versions offer something for everyone: from the traditional favorite topped with ketchup to a hearty mushroom version and one with a bourbon glaze for the topping. These recipes are easily doubled or tripled to serve a larger crowd. These meatloaves are all equally good when served with mashed potatoes and gravy. Each of these recipes makes one small meatloaf in a small loaf pan or 4 x 6–inch (10 x 15–cm) Pyrex® dish. Double the recipe to fit a large loaf pan or an 8 x 8–inch (20 x 20–cm) baking dish.

Serves 2

Classic Meatloaf

2 tsp (10 ml) olive oil

1 small carrot, trimmed, peeled and minced

1 small onion, minced

1 rib celery, minced

2 cloves garlic, minced

1 package Beyond Meat® or Impossible™ meat

1 tsp onion powder

½ tsp garlic powder

1 tsp paprika

½ tsp coarse salt

½ tsp freshly ground black pepper

3 tbsp (12 g) finely minced parsley

¼ cup (27 g) regular or gluten-free breadcrumbs

⅓ cup (80 ml) ketchup

Traditional meatloaf is in the top five of homey American comfort foods. Topped with ketchup and served with mashed or roasted potatoes, this dish is excellent for a warming dinner and is also great for next-day leftovers tucked between two slices of crusty bread or a roll.

Preheat the oven to 350°F (177°C).

Make the meatloaf: Heat the olive oil in a small sauté pan and add the carrot, onion and celery. Cook for 5 to 6 minutes, or until the carrot begins to lightly brown and the onion begins to soften and become translucent. Add the garlic and cook 1 minute more. Set aside.

In a large bowl, combine the carrot mixture with the remaining meatloaf ingredients (except for the ketchup) and mix well with a rubber spatula or knead well with your hands. Scoop the meatloaf mixture into a small loaf pan or casserole dish that has been sprayed with cooking spray. Alternatively, you can divide the mixture into four equal portions and form into small football-shaped "loaves" for individual meatloaves.

Spoon the ketchup onto the meatloaf and smooth evenly. Bake for 15 to 20 minutes, or until firm.

Serve hot with a side of your choice.

Bourbon & Brown Sugar–Glazed Meatloaf

Serves 2

For the meatloaf

2 tsp (10 ml) safflower or other flavorless oil

1 small carrot, trimmed, peeled and minced

2 shallots, minced

2 cloves garlic, minced

1 package Beyond Meat® or Impossible™ meat

1 tsp onion powder

½ tsp garlic powder

1 tsp paprika

½ tsp coarse salt

¼ tsp cayenne pepper or more to taste

3 tbsp (12 g) finely minced parsley

¼ cup (27 g) regular or gluten-free breadcrumbs

For the bourbon and brown sugar glaze

½ cup (120 ml) ketchup

1 tbsp (14 g) dark brown sugar

1 tbsp (15 ml) Worcestershire sauce

1 tbsp (15 ml) bourbon

¼ tsp onion powder

The glaze on this meatloaf reminds me of good old-fashioned Southern barbecue. Mashed potatoes are always a good option, but consider cornbread, grits or even coleslaw for your sides.

Preheat the oven to 350°F (177°C).

Make the meatloaf: Heat the safflower oil in a small sauté pan and add the carrot. Cook for 5 to 6 minutes, or until the carrot begins to lightly brown. Add the shallots and garlic and cook 1 to 2 minutes more. Set aside.

In a large bowl, combine the shallot mixture with the remaining meatloaf ingredients and mix well with a rubber spatula or knead well with your hands. Scoop the meatloaf mixture into a small loaf pan or casserole dish that has been sprayed with cooking spray. Alternatively, you can divide the mixture into four equal portions and form into small football-shaped "loaves" for individual meatloaves.

Make the bourbon and brown sugar glaze: Combine all the ingredients in a small bowl and whisk well until combined. Spread the mixture evenly on top of the meatloaf and bake for 15 to 20 minutes, or until firm.

Serve hot with a side of your choice.

Mushroom Meatloaf

2 tsp (10 ml) olive oil

1 small carrot, trimmed, peeled and minced

1 small onion, minced

1 rib celery, minced

1 cup (230 g) sliced cremini mushrooms

2 cloves garlic, minced

1 tsp finely minced fresh thyme

1 package Beyond Meat® or Impossible™ meat

1 tsp onion powder

½ tsp garlic powder

1 tsp paprika

½ tsp coarse salt

½ tsp freshly ground black pepper

3 tbsp (12 g) finely minced parsley

¼ cup (27 g) regular or gluten-free breadcrumbs

2 tbsp (30 ml) Worcestershire sauce

⅓ cup (80 ml) ketchup

This meatloaf is a treat for mushroom lovers. While the recipe calls for cremini—the small brown mushrooms that are commonly available in most grocery stores—you can certainly substitute your favorite mushrooms.

Preheat the oven to 350°F (177°C).

Make the meatloaf: Heat the olive oil in a small sauté pan and add the carrot, onion and celery. Cook for 5 to 6 minutes, or until the carrot begins to lightly brown and the onion begins to soften and become translucent. Add the mushrooms, mix well and cook for 4 to 5 minutes more. Add the garlic and thyme leaves, cooking for 1 minute more. Set aside.

In a large bowl, combine the mushroom mixture with the remaining meatloaf ingredients except the Worcestershire sauce and the ketchup and mix well with a rubber spatula or knead well with your hands. Scoop the meatloaf mixture into a small loaf pan or casserole dish that has been sprayed with cooking spray. Alternatively, you can divide the mixture into four equal portions and form into small football-shaped "loaves" for individual meatloaves.

Make the topping: Mix the Worcestershire sauce and the ketchup in a small bowl, and spoon onto the meatloaf and smooth evenly. Bake for 20 to 25 minutes, or until firm.

Serve hot with a side of your choice.

Serves 6

Stuffed Tomatoes

6 large tomatoes

2 tsp (10 ml) safflower oil

½ small onion, minced

4 cloves garlic, minced

1 package Beyond Meat® or Impossible™ meat

½ cup (120 ml) plain tomato sauce

1 tsp salt

½ tsp freshly ground black pepper

½ cup (24 g) shredded fresh basil

½ cup (54 g) regular or gluten-free breadcrumbs

1 cup (112 g) shredded vegan mozzarella cheese

Vegan pesto, for garnish (optional)

Stuffed tomatoes are a delight in summer when vine-ripened tomatoes are to be had. Choose wide, fat tomatoes that are not too soft or they won't hold their shape. This recipe is enhanced by that perfect summer tomato accompaniment: fresh basil.

Preheat the oven to 350°F (177°C).

Using a small, sharp knife, slice around the top of the tomato in a small circle, angling the knife to cut into the tomato and pull out the top like a core. Use a small spoon to scrape out the tomato flesh through the top and into a small bowl. Repeat with all of the tomatoes and set aside.

Heat the safflower oil in a large frying pan over medium heat and add the onion. Fry until it begins to soften and become translucent, 5 to 6 minutes, then add the garlic and fry for 1 minute more. Add the alternative meat, breaking it up with a wooden spoon. Fry the alternative meat until it is lightly browned, about 6 minutes.

Stir in the tomato sauce and reserved tomato filling and cook for 6 to 7 minutes, or until the liquid is reduced by one-third. Add the salt, pepper and basil and mix well. Stir in the breadcrumbs.

Place the tomatoes on a baking sheet or in another oven-safe dish. Divide and spoon the meat mixture evenly among all the tomatoes. Bake for 10 minutes, then sprinkle the top of each tomato evenly with the cheese and bake for 7 to 8 minutes more, or until the cheese is melted.

Serve hot garnished with vegan pesto, if desired.

Serves 4 to 6

Jambalaya

1 tbsp (15 ml) safflower oil

1 small onion, minced

1 small green bell pepper, stemmed, seeded and minced

2 ribs celery, trimmed and minced

2 cloves garlic, minced

½ small red chili, stemmed, seeded and minced (optional)

1 cup (196 g) basmati rice

1 cup (240 ml) vegetable stock

1 (15-oz [425-g]) can crushed tomatoes

¼ tsp cayenne pepper

1 package Beyond Sausage® Hot Italian

1 cup (100 g) fresh or frozen okra, sliced

¼ cup (15 g) minced fresh parsley, for garnish

Jambalaya is a classic Cajun dish from New Orleans that begins with what is commonly called the holy trinity of New Orleanian cooking: onion, green bell pepper and celery. A one-pot meal that combines vegetables, rice and meats, jambalaya comes out of the tradition of West African jollof rice, French pilaf and Spanish paella—representing the various culinary styles that influenced the city's culture. Okra adds a little thickness to the sauce in this dish, but some may not like its "slimy" texture. You may omit if you don't care for it.

Heat the safflower oil in a large, deep frying pan or saucepan over medium heat. Add the onion, bell pepper and celery and fry for 5 to 6 minutes, or until the onion begins to soften and become translucent. Add the garlic and red chili, if using, and fry 1 minute more.

Wash the rice by placing it in a deep bowl and filling it with cold water. Swirl the water around with your hand until it is cloudy. Carefully drain the water. Repeat four or five times until the water is clear. Set aside.

Add the washed rice to the pan with the cooked vegetables. Stir in the vegetable stock, tomatoes and cayenne pepper. Reduce heat to a simmer and cook for 15 minutes, stirring once or twice.

While the vegetables are simmering, cook the alternative meat: Spray a large frying pan with cooking spray and cook the alternative meat over medium heat. Fry 6 to 7 minutes, turning every couple of minutes so the sausage is brown on all sides. Remove from the heat and allow to cool. When the sausage is cool enough to handle, slice each one diagonally into ½-inch (1.3-cm) slices.

Add the sausage slices and the okra to the rice mixture and simmer for 5 to 7 minutes more, or until the liquid is almost completely absorbed.

Serve garnished with chopped parsley.

Shepherd's Pie

For the mashed potatoes

1 tsp salt, plus more to taste

3 large russet potatoes, peeled

2 tsp (10 g) butter or vegan butter

¼ cup (60 ml) unsweetened milk or plant-based milk

Freshly ground pepper to taste

For the filling

1 tbsp (15 ml) olive oil

1 small carrot, peeled, trimmed and diced small

1 small onion, minced

½ lb (227 g) cremini mushrooms, diced small

1 clove garlic, minced

1 lb (454 g) Beyond Beef® Crumbles

1 tsp tomato paste

1 tsp pimenton

½ tsp ground cumin

¼ tsp allspice

2 tsp (10 ml) Worcestershire sauce

½ cup (120 ml) vegetable stock

¼ cup (60 ml) Guinness®

⅓ cup (48 g) fresh peas

Salt to taste

Freshly ground pepper to taste

Paprika, for garnish

This classic Irish recipe is a hearty one-dish meal than can be made ahead to be rewarmed in the oven just before serving. I like to use Beyond Beef® Crumbles because they have the texture to stand up to multiple rounds of cooking: frying, simmering and baking. The key to the fluffiest mashed potatoes is to put them through a potato ricer or food mill, if possible. Fresh peas are preferable in this recipe because they retain their bite and flavor, but frozen peas will work in a pinch.

Make the mashed potatoes: Bring 4 cups (960 ml) of water and 1 teaspoon of salt to a boil in a large saucepan and add the potatoes. Lower to a simmer and cook until the potatoes are fork-tender, 20 to 25 minutes. Drain the potatoes, reserving about ¼ cup (60 ml) of the boiling water.

Using a potato ricer or food mill, rice the potatoes into the pot with the remaining cooking water. Add the butter and mix well, until melted. Add the milk and salt and pepper to taste and place over low heat. Mix vigorously with a wooden spoon until the potatoes are smooth and creamy. Set aside.

Make the filling: Heat the olive oil in a large, deep frying pan or Dutch oven and add the carrot. Cook for 6 to 7 minutes, or until the carrot begins to brown, then add the onion. Cook for 5 to 6 minutes, or until the onion begins to soften and become translucent, then add the mushrooms and fry until lightly brown, 4 to 5 minutes. Add the garlic and fry 1 minute more.

Add the alternative meat and break it up using a wooden spoon. Brown the crumbles, mixing well with the other ingredients. Stir in the tomato paste, pimenton, cumin and allspice and cook for 1 to 2 minutes, stirring. Add the Worcestershire sauce, vegetable stock and stout and mix well. Simmer until the mixture is reduced by one-third, about 5 minutes, and then stir in the peas. Season with salt and pepper to taste and mix well.

Preheat the oven to 350°F (177°C). Pour the meat mixture into an 8 x 8–inch (20 x 20–cm) casserole or Pyrex® dish. Scrape the mashed potato topping over it, smoothing over the entire surface of the filling mixture with the back of the spoon or with a tiny offset spatula. Sprinkle the top with paprika.

Bake the shepherd's pie for 15 minutes, or until the edges of the potatoes begin to lightly brown. Alternatively, you may cover the casserole with tinfoil and refrigerate overnight before baking and serving. Serve hot.

CHAPTER 2

Latino-Caribbean Flavors

All-Out Nachos

For the pico de gallo

4 plum tomatoes, cored and diced

½ small red onion, minced

1 tbsp (4 g) minced fresh cilantro

1 clove garlic, minced

Juice of 1 lime

⅛ tsp ground cumin

¼ tsp coarse salt

Freshly ground black pepper to taste

For the nachos

2 tbsp (30 ml) olive oil

1 medium onion, minced

4 cloves garlic, minced

1 package Beyond Beef® Feisty Crumbles

1 tbsp (9 g) taco seasoning of your choice

1 tsp salt

1½ cups (363 g) canned diced fire-roasted tomatoes with jalapeño or 1½ cups (363 g) canned diced tomatoes plus 1 small jalapeño stemmed, seeded and chopped small

1 bag large tortilla chips

2 cups (226 g) shredded vegan cheddar cheese

1 small jalapeño, thinly sliced (optional)

3 tbsp (12 g) minced fresh cilantro

Vegan sour cream, for serving (optional)

In order to bring out the best flavor, it's important to take the time to brown the alternative meat well in this recipe. Gooey, melty cheese is key to any good nacho recipe. I like Daiya brand "cheeses" for this version—as well as most recipes calling for cheese—because of their taste and melting quality.

Make the pico de gallo: Mix all the ingredients together in a bowl and refrigerate for at least 30 minutes.

Make the nachos: Heat the olive oil in a large skillet over medium heat and add the onion. Fry the onion for 5 to 6 minutes, or until it begins to soften and become translucent. Add the garlic and fry 1 to 2 minutes more. Add the alternative meat to the pan and use a wooden spoon to break up the crumbles, frying for 5 to 6 minutes.

Add the taco seasoning and salt and mix well. Fry 1 minute more, then stir in the tomatoes with jalapeño and cook until most of the liquid is absorbed, 5 to 6 minutes.

Layer the tortilla chips on the bottom of a large baking dish and spread the cooked crumble mixture over the top. Spread the cheese on top of the crumbles, then sprinkle the jalapeño, if using, on top of the cheese.

Heat the oven on the broil setting. Place the dish in the oven and cook until the cheese is melted and bubbling, 4 to 5 minutes. Remove from the oven.

Evenly spread the pico de gallo on the chips along with some cilantro and a dollop of sour cream, if using. Serve hot.

Zesty Quesadillas

2 tbsp (30 ml) olive oil

1 small onion, minced

4 cloves garlic, minced

2 packages (566 g) Beyond Beef® Feisty Crumbles

1 tbsp (9 g) taco seasoning of your choice

½ tsp salt

1 plum tomato, cored and chopped small

2 to 3 tbsp (8 to 12 g) minced fresh cilantro

16 large tortillas

2 cups (226 g) shredded vegan cheddar cheese

Pico de gallo (page 48), for serving

Guacamole, for serving

Vegan sour cream, for serving

Salsa, for serving

Quesadillas are versatile enough to eat as a whole meal or can be sliced into smaller pieces for appetizers. Serve these quesadillas with the salsa of your choice, guacamole and plant-based sour cream. I find that Beyond Beef® Feisty Crumbles work well with this recipe because they're already well-seasoned for this flavor profile.

Heat the olive oil in a large skillet over medium heat and add the onion. Fry for 4 to 5 minutes, until it begins to soften and become translucent. Add the garlic and fry 1 to 2 minutes more. Add the alternative meat and use a wooden spoon to break the crumbles up into small pieces, frying for 5 to 6 minutes.

Add the taco seasoning and salt and mix well. Fry 1 minute more, then add the tomato and cook 2 to 3 minutes. Stir in the cilantro and set aside.

Spray another large skillet with cooking spray over medium-low heat and add one of the tortillas. Toast for 1 minute and flip over and toast the other side. Repeat with all of the tortillas and set aside.

Return one of the tortillas to the skillet and spoon 3 to 4 tablespoons (45 to 60 g) of the meat mixture onto the tortilla and then top evenly with ¼ cup (28 g) of cheese. Place another toasted tortilla on top and cover the skillet with a lid.

Cook for 1 to 2 minutes, or until the cheese begins to melt, and use a wide spatula to flip over the quesadilla. Cook for 1 to 2 minutes and remove. Repeat the process with the remaining tortillas, meat mixture and cheese.

Using a pizza cutter or a sharp chef's knife, cut each quesadilla into four, six or eight pieces, depending on your preference.

Serve with pico de gallo, guacamole, sour cream and salsa.

Tacos

2 tbsp (30 ml) olive oil

1 small onion, minced

4 cloves garlic, minced

2 packages Beyond Beef® Feisty Crumbles

1 tbsp (9 g) taco seasoning of your choice

1 tsp salt

1 cup (240 ml) plain tomato sauce

3 tbsp (12 g) minced fresh cilantro

8 small tortillas or corn taco shells

Pico de gallo (page 48), for serving

Guacamole, for serving

Shredded vegan cheddar cheese, for serving

Vegan sour cream, for serving

Salsa, for serving

I like to make taco filling with Beyond Beef® Feisty Crumbles, but you can use the regular Beyond Meat® or Impossible™ "raw" meats as well. Tacos are a perfect self-serve meal—I put out all the fixings and allow people to make their own. I put out guacamole, pico de gallo (page 48), vegan sour cream and vegan shredded cheese. Fire-roasted and green salsa nicely round out the offerings. While I offer guests a choice between soft corn or flour tortillas and crunchy shells, you can decide what you like best.

Heat the olive oil in a large skillet over medium heat and add the onion. Fry for 5 to 6 minutes, until the onion begins to soften and become translucent. Add the garlic and fry 1 to 2 minutes more.

Add the alternative meat and, using a wooden spoon, break it up into small pieces, frying for 5 to 6 minutes, until browned.

Add the taco seasoning and salt and mix well. Fry 1 minute more, then add the tomato sauce and cook 2 to 3 minutes to slightly thicken.

Stir in the cilantro and serve hot in tortillas or taco shells with pico de gallo, guacamole, cheese, sour cream and salsa.

Serves 8 to 10

Enchilada Dip

2 tsp (10 ml) safflower oil

1 medium onion, minced

3 cloves garlic, minced

1 package Beyond Meat® or Impossible™ meat

2 plum tomatoes, cored and chopped

15 oz (444 ml) or about 2 cups (480 ml) enchilada sauce

1 cup (260 g) canned or reconstituted dried pinto beans (see page 14)

1 tsp salt

2 cups (226 g) shredded vegan cheddar cheese

1 to 2 tbsp (4 to 8 g) chopped fresh cilantro

Tortilla chips, for serving

This dip has all the flavors of classic enchiladas, plus it's scoopable with a tortilla chip. Popular for Super Bowl parties, this dip eats like a meal and can even sub for a fun and fast dinner.

Preheat the oven to 350°F (177°C). Heat the safflower oil in a large frying pan over medium heat and add the onion. Fry until the onion begins to soften and become translucent, 6 to 7 minutes, then add the garlic and fry for 1 minute more.

Add the alternative meat and use a wooden spoon to break it up, frying for 6 to 7 minutes or until browned. Stir in the tomatoes and cook for 3 minutes, then add the enchilada sauce and mix well.

Mix in the beans and salt and simmer for 1 to 2 minutes more. Spoon the bean mixture into an 8 x 8–inch (20 x 20–cm) baking dish and top with the cheese. Bake in the preheated oven for 10 to 12 minutes, or until the cheese melts.

Top with fresh cilantro and serve with tortilla chips.

Enchiladas

Serves 4

2 tsp (10 ml) safflower oil

1 medium onion, minced

3 cloves garlic, minced

1 package Beyond Meat® or Impossible™ meat

2 plum tomatoes, cored and chopped

15 oz (444 ml) enchilada sauce, divided

1 tsp salt

8 large tortillas

2 cups (226 g) shredded vegan cheddar cheese

1 to 2 tbsp (4 to 8 g) chopped fresh cilantro, for garnish

Enchiladas are gooey, spicy and delicious. Yellow rice or rice and beans are excellent side dishes for these saucy treats.

Preheat the oven to 350°F (177°C). Heat the safflower oil in a large frying pan over medium heat and add the onion. Fry until the onion begins to soften and become translucent, 4 to 5 minutes, then add the garlic and fry for 1 minute more.

Add the alternative meat and use a wooden spoon to break it up, frying for 5 to 6 minutes or until browned. Stir in the tomatoes and cook for 3 minutes, then add half of the enchilada sauce and the salt and mix well.

Have a large casserole dish ready. Pour half of the remaining enchilada sauce in the bottom of the dish. Spoon about one-eighth of the meat mixture onto one side of a tortilla. Roll the tortilla forward into a cylinder and place it, seam side down, in the dish. Repeat until all the filling and tortillas are used.

Pour the remaining enchilada sauce over the enchiladas and top with cheese. Bake in the preheated oven for 10 to 12 minutes, or until the cheese melts. Serve hot garnished with cilantro.

Picadillo

Serves 4

2 tsp (10 ml) safflower oil

1 medium onion, minced

4 ají dulce peppers or 1 medium bell pepper, stemmed, seeded and minced

3 cloves garlic, minced

1 package Beyond Meat® or Impossible™ meat

1 tsp salt

½ tsp freshly ground black pepper or to taste

½ tsp ground cumin

½ tsp cilantro

½ tsp ground coriander

½ tsp cayenne pepper

2 plum tomatoes, cored and chopped

1 cup (240 ml) tomato sauce

½ cup (73 g) golden raisins

½ cup (90 g) green olives, sliced

1 tbsp (9 g) capers

1 tbsp (14 g) dark brown sugar

Picadillo is a minced meat dish that is common throughout Hispanic countries, with slight variations based on region. The best way to describe picadillo is as a dish with a lot going on—including some surprising pairings like olives and raisins—but always with a delicious result. Picadillo is served regularly with rice but also as a taco or empanada filling. A similar filling is used in some Latinx nations for steamed corn turnovers like tamales. Serve with cooked rice.

Heat the safflower oil in a large frying pan over medium heat and add the onion and peppers. Fry until the onion begins to soften and become translucent, 6 to 7 minutes, then add the garlic and fry 1 minute more.

Add the alternative meat and use a wooden spoon to break it up, frying for 5 to 6 minutes or until browned. Add the salt, pepper, cumin, cilantro, coriander and cayenne pepper and mix well.

Stir in the tomatoes and tomato sauce. Cook for 3 minutes, then add the raisins, olives, capers and brown sugar. Reduce heat to a simmer and cook for 2 minutes more. Serve hot.

Three-Bean Spicy Chili Verde

½ cup (83 g) dried hominy or canned hominy

⅛ tsp baking soda

2 tbsp (30 ml) olive oil, divided

1 medium onion, chopped small

3 cloves garlic, minced

½ cup (90 g) cooked or canned Great Northern beans

½ cup (92 g) white kidney beans

½ cup (104 g) navy beans

2 cups (480 ml) vegetable stock

8 oz (237 ml) salsa verde of your choice

1 tsp salt

Freshly ground pepper to taste

2 lbs (904 g) Trader Joe's® Turkeyless Protein Patties

Chopped cilantro

1 small Haas avocado, sliced

1 small lime, sliced into wedges

This three-bean chili uses Turkeyless Protein Patties from Trader Joe's®, but you can also use the kind of chicken substitute that you reconstitute at home and shape into bite-size pieces before the frying step.

This chili also features hominy corn for a little extra "bite." Dried, reconstituted hominy gives a heartier texture to this chili, but canned hominy works just fine.

This is also a great slow cooker dish—simply add the turkey-less or chicken-less pieces just before serving. Adjust the spice level to your liking by choosing a mild, medium or hot salsa verde. If you like, you can really turn up the heat with the addition of some canned Hatch chiles. Serve this chili on its own or with cornbread or rice.

If using dried hominy, reconstitute it by soaking it overnight in a large bowl in 6 cups (1.4 L) of water. Drain the water and bring 6 cups (1.4 L) of water to a boil in a large pot with the baking soda. Add the hominy and lower to a simmer. Simmer for 20 to 30 minutes, or until the hominy is tender. Alternatively, you can reconstitute the hominy using a pressure cooker if you have one. Add the hominy to an Instant Pot® or other pressure cooker with 6 cups (1.4 L) of water and the baking soda. Cook under pressure for 20 minutes. Release pressure carefully and drain. Set aside.

Heat a large pot with 1 tablespoon (15 ml) of the olive oil and add the onion. Fry until it begins to soften and become translucent, 6 to 7 minutes, then add the garlic. Fry for 30 seconds more.

Add the beans and hominy to the pan along with the vegetable stock, salsa verde, salt and pepper. Stir well and allow to simmer for 30 to 40 minutes, or until the liquid is reduced by two-thirds.

While the beans are simmering, form the alternative meat into small flat nuggets, about 1 inch (2.5 cm) in size. Heat a large skillet over medium-low heat and add the remaining 1 tablespoon (15 ml) of oil. Add the nuggets and brown lightly on both sides, 1 to 2 minutes. Remove and set aside.

Add the nuggets and beans to the bean mixture and simmer for 4 to 5 minutes more.

Serve the chili in individual bowls. Sprinkle with cilantro and add a few slices of avocado to each. Place a lime wedge on top to serve.

Mexican-Style Stuffed Poblanos

4 poblano peppers

2 tsp (10 ml) safflower oil

½ small onion, minced

4 cloves garlic, minced

1 package Beyond Meat® or Impossible™ meat

1 tsp ground cumin

½ tsp ground coriander

1 tsp salt

½ tsp freshly ground black pepper

1 (15-oz [425-g]) can diced fire-roasted tomatoes with jalapeño

1 cup (172 g) cooked black beans (see page 14)

1 cup (165 g) fire-roasted corn niblets

½ cup (80 g) cooked rice

2 cups (226 g) shredded vegan cheddar cheese

Poblano peppers are hot enough for a nice kick that still allows a bell pepper flavor to come through, but not so hot that they are unpleasant to eat. You will still want to keep some white vinegar handy to wash your hands and surfaces when stemming and seeding these peppers because the seeds are where the heat lies. I like to use a longer-grain rice like basmati for the filling and fire-roasted corn kernels, which you can find frozen in most grocery stores.

Preheat the oven to 350°F (177°C).

Using a small, sharp knife, slice each poblano pepper in half, leaving the stems intact, from stem to bottom. Using your knife, cut out the seed bed from the stem and discard. Rinse the pepper under running water to remove any stray seeds. Repeat with all the peppers and set aside.

Heat the safflower oil in a large frying pan over medium heat and add the onion. Fry until it begins to soften and become translucent, 5 to 6 minutes, then add the garlic and fry for 1 minute more. Add the alternative meat, breaking it up with a wooden spoon. Fry the alternative meat until it is lightly browned, about 6 minutes.

Stir in the cumin, coriander, salt and pepper and add the tomatoes, black beans and corn and mix well. Cook for 3 to 4 minutes, or until most of the liquid is absorbed. Turn off the heat and stir in the cooked rice.

Place the peppers on a baking sheet or in another oven-safe dish. Divide and spoon the meat mixture evenly among all the peppers. Bake for 10 minutes, then sprinkle the top of each poblano evenly with the cheese and bake for 7 to 8 minutes more, or until the cheese is melted. Serve hot.

Makes 12

Jamaican-Style Patties

For the crust

3 cups (375 g) white flour

2½ sticks (568 g) shortening, cut into small cubes

1½ tsp (9 g) salt

Ice water, as needed

For the filling

2 tsp (10 ml) safflower oil

1 small onion, minced

1 cup (205 g) grated calabaza (Caribbean pumpkin) or butternut squash

2 cloves garlic, minced

2 scallions, ends trimmed and minced

¼ scotch bonnet pepper, minced

1½ tsp (1.5 g) fresh thyme leaves

1 lb (454 g) Beyond Beef® Crumbles, defrosted

2 tsp (5 g) madras curry powder

1 tsp dark brown sugar

1 slice bread soaked in ¼ cup (60 ml) water

For the annatto oil

⅓ cup (80 ml) safflower oil

1 tsp annatto seeds

Beef patties, or just "patties," are a pan-Caribbean favorite most often credited to Jamaica. These handheld pies were the original portable "fast" food, but today they serve very well as a quick snack or appetizer, and coupled with a salad or soup, they can make for a filling meal. I use the Beyond Beef® Crumbles in this recipe because they are already cooked and can simply be mixed with the other ingredients, retaining the right texture for baking inside the pastry crust. Premade empanada crusts make this otherwise laborious dish easier to prepare; however, no one could fault you for preferring homemade crust—and that recipe is included as well. Don't skimp on the annatto oil if you can help it. This is what gives it the rich yellow color and slight tang that makes Jamaican patties so recognizable.

Make the crust: Place the flour, shortening and salt in a food processor and pulse until the shortening is the size of peas, then pour the mixture into a large bowl. Alternatively, you may place the ingredients in a large bowl and use a pastry cutter or sturdy fork to achieve the same consistency.

Add the ice water 1 tablespoon (15 ml) at a time to the flour mixture and stir with a wooden spoon until the mixture just comes together. Wrap in plastic wrap and chill for 60 minutes. Remove the dough from the refrigerator, cut it into 12 equal-sized pieces and roll each piece quickly into a ball between your palms. Roll each ball into a disc about 6 inches (15 cm) wide. Keep the dough balls chilled as you roll them out, then return the discs to the refrigerator. If you are using premade empanada discs, lightly roll them into a 6-inch (15-cm) circle.

Make the filling: Heat the safflower oil in a large, deep frying pan and add the onion. Fry for 4 to 5 minutes, or until the onion begins to soften and become translucent. Add the calabaza or butternut squash and cook 6 to 7 minutes. Add the garlic, scallions, scotch bonnet pepper and thyme and cook 1 to 2 minutes.

Remove the filling from the heat and cool. Stir in the alternative meat, madras curry powder, brown sugar and water-soaked bread and mix well. You will be able to easily mold the mixture into a ball shape.

Make the annatto oil: In a small saucepan, heat the safflower oil over low heat and add the annatto seeds. Heat until the seeds release all of their dark orange color, 5 to 6 minutes. Do not allow the seeds to burn. Strain out the seeds and set the oil aside.

Assemble the patties: Place a dough disc on a lightly floured work surface and place 1 generous tablespoon (18 g) of filling on one side, leaving about a ¼ inch (6 mm) border from the edge of the dough. Brush the edge of the dough disc with water, then fold the unfilled side of the dough disc over the filled side to form a half-moon. Using a fork, press the edges of the dough together. Prick the top of the finished patty once or twice with a fork. Repeat with all the dough and filling.

Brush each finished patty with annatto oil, making sure that the surface is totally covered and deeply orange. Chill the pies, covered with plastic, for 30 minutes. At this stage, the pies can be individually frozen and then stored in a zip-top bag in the freezer.

Preheat the oven to 350°F (177°C). Place the patties on a cookie sheet about 1 inch (2.5 cm) apart on all sides. Bake for 20 to 25 minutes, or until the crust is golden brown. Serve hot.

Tamale Pie

For the filling

1 tbsp (15 ml) olive oil

1 small onion, minced

3 cloves garlic, minced

¾ package Beyond Meat® or Impossible™ meat

1 tbsp (9 g) taco seasoning of your choice

1 tbsp (16 g) tomato paste

1 (15-oz [425-g]) can crushed tomatoes

1 tsp salt

½ tsp freshly ground black pepper

¼ tsp cayenne pepper (optional)

4 slices vegan provolone

4 slices vegan cheddar cheese

For the topping

¾ cup (92 g) cornmeal

¾ cup (94 g) flour

⅔ cup (132 g) granulated sugar

½ tsp kosher salt

½ tsp baking soda

½ cup (114 g) vegan butter, melted

Vegan egg replacer equal to 2 eggs

1 cup (240 ml) almond milk or other vegan milk alternative

Vegan sour cream, for serving (optional)

Guacamole, for serving (optional)

Tamale pie puts all the good things that make a traditional tamale in one baked casserole: cornmeal crust, spiced ground meat and cheese. Use whichever powdered taco seasoning you prefer so you can decide your level of heat. Taco seasoning sauces work well, too, but if you use them, omit the tomato paste and reduce the amount of crushed tomatoes accordingly.

Preheat the oven to 350°F (177°C).

Make the filling: Heat the olive oil in a large frying pan over medium heat. Add the onion and fry 4 to 5 minutes, or until it begins to soften and become translucent. Add the garlic and mix well. Fry for 1 minute more.

Add the alternative meat and use a wooden spoon to break it up. Fry for 6 to 7 minutes, or until browned. Sprinkle with taco seasoning and cook for 1 minute, then add the tomato paste and stir well, cooking for 1 minute more.

Stir in the tomatoes, salt, pepper and cayenne pepper, if using. Simmer for 5 to 6 minutes and pour into an 8 x 8–inch (20 x 20–cm) baking dish.

Layer the cheese over the top of the meat mixture. Set aside.

Make the topping: Whisk together the cornmeal, flour, sugar, salt and baking soda. In another bowl, combine the butter, egg replacer and milk alternative. Whisk well.

Add the dry ingredients to the wet and beat well with a wooden spoon. Pour the batter over the top of the meat and cheese mixture and bake the tamale pie for 30 to 35 minutes, or until the top is golden brown, firm and a cake tester comes out clean.

Serve with sour cream and guacamole to garnish, if desired.

CHAPTER 3

Eastern Flavors (Asia & India)

Korean-Style Egg Rolls

For the egg rolls

2 tsp (10 ml) toasted sesame oil, divided

2 tbsp (30 ml) safflower oil, divided, plus more for frying

½ small onion, minced

1 cup (210 g) minced shiitake mushrooms

2 cloves garlic, minced

1 tbsp (15 g) grated ginger

1 cup (70 g) shredded cabbage

1 carrot, peeled, trimmed and julienned

1 package Impossible™ meat

2 tsp (10 g) Gochujang chili paste or ¼ cup (60 ml) hoisin sauce

¼ cup (60 ml) soy sauce

1 package vegan egg roll wrappers

I chose a Korean-style spice mix for these egg rolls—which means they are spicy. If you don't like heat, you can substitute hoisin sauce for the Gochujang paste and this will give you a sweeter flavor profile. This recipe can be made ahead as far as rolling the egg rolls to fry just before serving. Freeze for up to 1 month. You can make them up to 24 hours ahead. If you do so, fry them frozen.

Make the egg roll filling: Heat a large frying pan over medium heat and add half the sesame oil and half the safflower oil. Add the onion and fry 4 to 5 minutes, until it begins to soften and become translucent.

Add the mushrooms and stir well. Cook for 3 to 4 minutes, or until lightly browned, then add the garlic and ginger. Fry for 1 minute more.

Stir in the cabbage and carrot and fry for 2 to 3 minutes. Scrape the mixture into a large bowl.

Add the remaining oil to the frying pan and heat over medium heat. Add the alternative meat and break it up with a wooden spoon. Fry 6 to 7 minutes, until browned. Stir in the Gochujang paste and soy sauce. Mix well and cook for 1 to 2 minutes more, until almost all the liquid is absorbed.

Add the meat mixture to the bowl with the mushroom and cabbage mixture and mix very well. Set aside until cool.

Form the egg rolls: Hold an egg roll wrapper in front of you like a diamond. Use your finger and wet all the edges of all sides of the wrapper. Place 2 or 3 tablespoons (30 or 45 g) of filling just off center on the wrapper, leaving about 1 inch (2.5 cm) on each end.

Fold the short sides in over the filling, as if you were wrapping a present. Fold the right side of the wrapper over the filling and roll forward, away from you, like a burrito, pressing gently so the edge of the egg roll is tightly sealed. Repeat with the remaining wrappers.

Heat a large frying pan with about 2 inches (5 cm) of safflower oil until hot. Test the oil by dropping a small piece of an egg roll wrapper in the oil. If it immediately bubbles and fries, the oil is ready.

(continued)

Korean-Style Egg Rolls (cont.)

For the dipping sauce

¼ cup (60 ml) soy sauce

¼ cup (60 ml) rice wine vinegar

1 tbsp (14 g) brown sugar

1 tbsp (15 ml) toasted sesame oil

⅛ tsp powdered ginger

⅛ tsp freshly ground pepper

1 tsp cornstarch mixed with 1 tbsp (15 ml) water

Gently place the egg rolls in the frying pan, leaving 1 to 2 inches (2.5 to 5 cm) of space around each. Fry each egg roll for 1 to 2 minutes, until they bubble and are golden brown. Using tongs, turn the egg rolls over and fry 1 to 2 minutes more. Remove from the oil and place on a plate with doubled-up paper towels or on a wire rack over a cookie sheet.

Make the dipping sauce: Combine all the ingredients except for the cornstarch and water in a small saucepan over medium-low heat. Bring to a low simmer until all the sugar is dissolved, 4 to 5 minutes.

Add the cornstarch mixture and stir well. Simmer for 1 to 2 minutes, or until slightly thickened.

Serve the egg rolls hot with the dipping sauce.

Indian Meat Samosas

For the dough

3 cups (375 g) white flour

2½ sticks (568 g) shortening or vegan butter, cut into small cubes

1½ tsp (9 g) salt

Ice water, as needed

Spicy with a meat filling that includes potatoes and peas, samosas are a popular Indian restaurant appetizer that can be hearty enough for a meal in and of themselves. All-veg, frozen versions can be found in many mainstream grocers, but it's easy enough to make your own and freeze for when you need them at a later date. Defrost in the refrigerator before frying.

Make the dough: If using homemade crust, place the flour, shortening and salt in a food processor and pulse until the shortening is the size of peas, then pour into a large bowl. Alternatively, you may place the ingredients in a large bowl and use a pastry cutter or sturdy fork to achieve the same consistency.

Add the ice water 1 tablespoon (15 ml) at a time to the flour mixture and stir with a wooden spoon until the mixture just comes together. Wrap in plastic wrap and chill for 60 minutes.

Remove the dough from the refrigerator and cut it into 12 equal-sized pieces. Roll each piece quickly into a ball between your palms. Roll each ball into a disc about 6 inches (15 cm) wide. Keep the dough balls chilled before you roll them out, then return the discs to the refrigerator.

(continued)

Indian Meat Samosas (cont.)

For the filling

2 tsp (10 ml) safflower oil, plus 3 cups (720 ml) for frying, divided

1 small onion, minced

2 scallions, ends trimmed and minced

2 cloves garlic, minced

¼ red chili pepper, minced

1 lb (454 g) Beyond Beef® Crumbles

2 tsp (3 g) garam masala

1 tsp turmeric powder

1 tsp salt

1 cup (145 g) fresh or frozen peas

1 russet potato, peeled and cut into small cubes

Tamarind Sauce (page 76), for serving

Cilantro Dipping Sauce (page 79), for serving

Make the filling: Heat the safflower oil in a large, deep frying pan and add the onion. Fry for 4 to 5 minutes, or until it begins to soften and become translucent. Add the scallions, garlic and pepper and cook for 1 to 2 minutes.

Add the alternative meat and break it up with a wooden spoon. Add the garam masala, turmeric and salt and mix well, cooking for 5 to 6 minutes more. Add the peas and potatoes along with 1 cup (240 ml) of water. Cover and reduce heat to a simmer for 15 minutes, or until the potatoes just soften. Remove from the heat and cool.

Assemble the samosas: Place a dough disc on a lightly floured work surface and place 1 generous tablespoon (16 g) of filling on one side, leaving about a one quarter-inch border from the edge of the dough. Brush the edge of the dough disc with water, then pinch the dough together halfway along the disc, leaving the other side open. Fold up the remaining side of the disc perpendicular to the seam you've already made and pinch this seam to the original seam. You will have a stuffed pastry that is shaped like a fat pyramid. Repeat with all the dough and filling.

Chill the samosas, covered with plastic, for 30 minutes. At this stage, the pies can be individually frozen and then stored in a zip-top bag in the freezer.

Cook the samosas: Heat the safflower oil in a large, deep saucepan on medium heat until a pinch of flour added to the oil sizzles immediately, about 8 minutes. Add the samosas carefully to the hot oil, working in batches so you do not crowd the pan. Fry for 3 to 4 minutes, or until golden brown on all sides. Remove with a slotted spoon and place on a sheet tray with a wire rack set over it or lined with paper towels.

Alternatively, you may bake the samosas: Preheat the oven to 350°F (177°C). Spray a cookie sheet with baking spray and place the samosas about 1 inch (2.5 cm) apart on all sides. Bake for 20 to 25 minutes, or until the crust is golden brown.

Serve hot with Tamarind Sauce and Cilantro Dipping Sauce.

Tamarind Sauce

1 tsp safflower oil

1 small shallot, minced

1 clove garlic, minced

1 small chili pepper, stemmed, seeded and minced

1¼ cups (300 ml) water

5 tbsp (75 ml) tamarind concentrate (available in Asian and Middle Eastern grocery stores)

½ cup (110 g) brown sugar

This sweet-tart sauce is a classic samosa sauce and also works well drizzled on grilled vegetables or even as a dipping sauce for chicken wings. The chili pepper gives it a good bite, but if you aren't a fan of hot and spicy sauces, you can omit it and still have a lovely sweet and sour sauce for a variety of uses.

Heat the safflower oil in a small saucepan over medium heat, add the shallot, garlic and pepper and fry for 1 minute.

Add the water and bring it to a boil, then add the tamarind concentrate and brown sugar. Mix very well and reduce heat to a simmer. Simmer until reduced by half, or until it is a syrup thick enough to coat the back of a spoon, about 8 minutes. Cool completely and serve as a dipping sauce.

Cilantro Dipping Sauce

1 cup (16 g) packed cilantro leaves

5 cloves garlic, whole

1 small chili pepper, stemmed and seeded

Zest and juice of 1 lime

1 tsp salt

¼ cup (60 ml) water or more as needed for a smooth paste

Most will be familiar with this recipe as a popular condiment gracing the tables of Indian restaurants. It's very good with meat turnovers or even Asian-style dumplings.

Place the cilantro, garlic and pepper in a food processor or high-powered blender and process into a rough chop. Add the lime zest, lime juice and salt and process again into a rough paste.

Gradually add the water while processing the herb mixture so you get a smooth, medium-thick sauce that can be easily poured. Use as a dipping sauce for samosas. Store leftovers in an airtight container in the refrigerator.

Makes 24

Chinese-Style Dumplings

For the dumplings

1 package Impossible™ meat

1 tsp grated ginger

1 tsp grated garlic

1 scallion, root end trimmed and finely minced

1 tbsp (4 g) minced fresh cilantro

1 tbsp (15 ml) soy sauce

1 tbsp (15 ml) mirin

½ tsp five-spice powder

½ tsp Szechuan pepper (optional)

24 round dumpling wrappers

1 tsp toasted sesame oil plus 1 tbsp (15 ml) safflower oil, mixed, for frying

For the sauce

½ cup (120 ml) soy sauce

1 tbsp (15 ml) mirin

1 tsp toasted sesame oil

1 tsp grated garlic

¼ tsp grated ginger

I like to use Impossible™ meat for the dumpling filling because I find the taste is a bit lighter—and, therefore, more "pork" like. I also find that the Impossible™ meat product retains the right texture in preparations when it is encased in dough and boiled, steamed or fried versus a direct cooking method. Five-spice powder and dumpling wrappers are traditional Chinese products that are available in most grocery stores.

You can freeze uncooked dumplings in a single layer on a sheet tray and then store in the freezer in a zip-top bag. Freeze up to one month.

In a medium bowl, mix the alternative meat, ginger, garlic, scallion, cilantro, soy sauce, mirin, five-spice powder and Szechuan pepper, if using, and mix very well to combine.

Place a dumpling wrapper on a flat work surface. Place a scant tablespoon (13 g) of the filling in the middle of the wrapper and then fold over. Pinch the dough closed and set aside. Repeat with the remaining wrappers.

Cook the dumplings: To steam them, place a steamer basket over a large pot of boiling water and add the dumplings in a single layer. Steam for 10 to 12 minutes.

To fry them, place a large frying pan over medium heat and add half of the sesame oil and safflower oil mixture. Add the dumplings in a single layer, making sure not to crowd the pan. Fry 2 to 3 minutes on each side, or until golden brown. Add ¼ cup (60 ml) of water and cover the pan. Cook for 5 minutes, or until the water is evaporated. Remove and repeat with the remaining dumplings.

Make the dipping sauce: Combine all of the ingredients and serve with hot dumplings.

Serves 4 to 6

Shroom Lettuce Cups

1 tsp safflower oil

1 rib celery, washed, trimmed and chopped small

1 carrot, peeled, trimmed and chopped small

1 small onion, minced

3 cloves garlic, minced

8 shiitake mushrooms, chopped small

1 package Beyond Meat® or Impossible™ meat

½ tsp five-spice powder

2 tbsp (30 ml) hoisin sauce

1 tbsp (15 ml) soy sauce

½ cup (73 g) roasted peanuts, roughly chopped

2 tbsp (8 g) chopped fresh cilantro

1 head butter lettuce, leaves removed, rinsed and dried

These delightful lettuce cups have all the fun of a taco, only lighter. They are ideal for those avoiding starch-based burrito or taco shells.

Heat the safflower oil in a large frying pan over medium heat and add the celery and carrot. Cook for 4 to 5 minutes, then add the onion and garlic and cook for 4 to 5 minutes more. Add the mushrooms and stir well. Cook for 1 to 2 minutes.

Add the alternative meat and break it up, mixing well with the other ingredients. Fry well until the meat is browned, 6 to 7 minutes.

Add the five-spice powder and mix well, then stir in the hoisin sauce and soy sauce. Cook for 1 minute more and remove from the heat.

Stir in the peanuts and cilantro and serve with washed lettuce leaves. Add 1 tablespoon (15 g) of the meat mixture to 1 large lettuce leaf. Wrap the leaves up like a taco.

Serves 6

Wonton Soup

For the wontons

½ lb (227 g) Impossible™ meat

1 scallion, trimmed and finely chopped

5 to 6 shiitake mushrooms, minced

2 cloves garlic, finely chopped

½ fresh hot red chili pepper, finely chopped

1 tsp soy sauce

24 vegan wonton skins

For the soup broth

1 quart (960 ml) vegetable stock

1 scallion, chopped

1½-inch (4-cm) piece ginger, sliced

2 cloves garlic, sliced

1 tsp soy sauce

½ tsp toasted sesame oil

Salt to taste

White pepper to taste

5 stalks Chinese broccoli or baby bok choy

This is a vegan version of the popular Chinese restaurant soup. As with other recipes that call for raw "meat" encased in dough, I suggest using Impossible™ meat over Beyond Beef®. You can scale up the recipe for the wontons and then freeze them in a single layer. If you cook the wontons from frozen, add three minutes to their cooking time.

Fried wontons are an excellent appetizer on their own. Simply fry the wontons in heated safflower oil for two to three minutes or until golden brown and serve with soy or other dipping sauce of your choice.

Make the wontons: Combine the alternative meat with the scallion, mushrooms, garlic, pepper and soy sauce and set aside.

Have a small bowl of cold water ready. Place a wonton skin flat on a work surface and put 1 teaspoon of the meat mixture in the middle of the square skin. Dip a finger in cold water and run it along the edges of the wonton skin (this will help the skin stick together when folded). Fold the skin in half over the meat to form a rectangle and pinch the edges together. Fold the rectangle over on itself lengthwise again. Fold the rectangle horizontally over the stuffed section of the rectangle so that the short ends meet each other. Wet your fingers slightly and pinch the lower folds of the short ends together, leaving the top folds free. Repeat until all the skins are filled or all the filling is used up. Set aside.

Make the soup: Combine all the ingredients in a medium saucepan and bring to a simmer. Simmer for 5 to 10 minutes so flavors combine.

Add the wontons to the soup and simmer for 4 to 5 minutes more so they are cooked through. Serve hot.

Thai-Style Red Curry Coconut Soup

Serves 4

For the meatballs

2 (8-oz [226-g]) packages Trader Joe's® Turkeyless Protein Patties

2 cloves garlic, grated

2 tsp (10 g) grated ginger

2 scallions, minced

1 tsp fish sauce

1 tsp minced galangal

½ tsp salt

½ tsp freshly ground black pepper

For the soup

1 shallot, minced

1 tsp Thai red curry paste

2 cups (480 ml) coconut milk

2 tsp (10 ml) fresh lime juice

1 tsp brown sugar

½ stalk lemongrass

3 tbsp (12 g) chopped cilantro, for garnish

1 lime, sliced into wedges, for garnish

This creamy, spicy soup is redolent with aromas of lemongrass and red curry. Galangal is a rhizome in the ginger family with a mild taste and is usually found pickled in salt brine in the Asian section of most grocery stores. Small meatballs stand in for slices of chicken in the traditional version. Add cellophane rice noodles for a heartier soup that can serve as a whole meal.

Make the meatballs: Combine all the ingredients in a large bowl and knead well with your hands until completely combined. Form into 36 gumball-sized balls.

Preheat the oven 350°F (177°C). Place the meatballs on a cookie sheet or baking tray and bake for 10 minutes, or until firm. Remove the meatballs from the oven and set aside.

Make the soup: Combine all the ingredients except the cilantro and lime in a medium saucepan over medium heat and bring to a simmer for 5 minutes.

Return the meatballs to the pan and simmer for an additional 2 to 3 minutes. Toss well to coat.

Serve hot, garnished with cilantro and lime wedges on the side.

Szechuan-Style String Beans & Ground Meat

1 tbsp (15 ml) toasted sesame oil, divided

1 tbsp (15 ml) safflower oil, divided

1 lb (454 g) green beans, trimmed

2 cloves garlic, minced

1 package Impossible™ meat

1 tsp salt

1 tsp freshly ground black pepper

2 tbsp (30 ml) hoisin sauce

¼ cup (60 ml) soy sauce

¼ cup (60 ml) vegetable stock

This Chinese dish is popular on restaurant menus and is amazingly simple to prepare. The original most often features ground pork as the meat of choice, although turkey and beef are sometimes used as well. Use Impossible™ meat for this recipe because it has a lighter texture and it tastes more similar to pork. Hoisin sauce is a key ingredient so don't forgo it—you'll find that it is available in most grocery stores. Serve this recipe with short-grain rice.

Heat half the sesame oil and half the safflower oil in a large frying pan over medium-high heat and add the green beans. Fry 5 to 6 minutes, or until the green beans begin to brown. Remove from the pan and set aside.

Add the remaining oil to the pan and add the garlic. Fry for 1 minute and add the alternative meat, using a wooden spoon to break up the chunks. Mix well and continue frying until browned, 6 to 7 minutes.

Stir in the salt, pepper, hoisin sauce and soy sauce and mix very well.

Return the green beans to the pan and add the vegetable stock. Mix well and simmer for 5 to 6 minutes more. Serve hot.

Mee Krob
(Thai-Style Rice Noodles)

Serves 4

For the sauce

2 tbsp (30 ml) tamarind syrup

2 tbsp (30 ml) fresh lime juice

3 tbsp (42 g) brown sugar

3 tbsp (45 ml) soy sauce

2 tsp (10 g) tomato paste

For the noodles

1½ cups (360 ml) safflower oil

8 oz (227 g) dried rice noodles

4 oz (114 g) firm tofu, cut into 1-inch (2.5-cm) cubes

JUST Egg alternative equal to 2 eggs

6 cloves garlic, minced

1 scallion, minced

1 fresh red Thai chili, trimmed and minced

1 package Impossible™ meat

1 cup (85 g) bean sprouts, rinsed, for garnish

4 tbsp (16 g) roughly chopped cilantro, for garnish

1 scallion, trimmed and thinly sliced, for garnish

1 fresh red chili, sliced, for garnish

Mee krob is a Thai dish that is a wonderful mixture of textures and flavors: crispy, soft, crunchy and saucy. Use thin rice vermicelli for this dish and Impossible™ meat, which has a lighter texture and flavor. You may reduce the amount of chili pepper—or increase it—according to your taste.

Make the sauce: Combine all of the ingredients in a small saucepan over medium heat. Bring to a simmer and cook for 5 to 6 minutes, or until slightly thickened. Set aside.

Make the noodles: Heat the safflower oil in wok or deep saucepan until it reaches 375°F (191°C). If you do not have an oil thermometer, you can test the temperature by dropping a piece of noodle into the oil. If it immediately bubbles and fries, the oil is ready.

Break up the rice noodles into 1-inch (2.5-cm) pieces and add it in batches to the oil, frying for 10 to 20 seconds or until the noodles puff up. Remove with a slotted spoon and place on a cookie sheet lined with paper towels. Set aside.

Next, fry the cubes of tofu in the oil. Fry in batches, so as not to crowd the pan, until the tofu is crispy and light brown, about 2 minutes. Remove with a slotted spoon and set aside on a plate or cookie sheet lined with paper towels.

Drizzle the egg substitute in a circular motion into the hot oil. When it puffs and browns, remove from the pan and place on a plate or cookie sheet lined with paper towels. When the egg cools, cut it into 1-inch (2.5-cm) pieces.

Drain all but 1 tablespoon (15 ml) of oil from the pan and add the garlic, scallion and chili. Fry for 1 minute and then add the alternative meat, breaking it up with a wooden spoon. Fry for 6 to 7 minutes, or until cooked through and lightly browned.

Place the fried noodles on a large platter. Add the meat mixture on top, followed by the tofu and then the egg pieces. Pour the sauce mixture over all of the ingredients.

Garnish with bean sprouts, cilantro, scallion and sliced chili pepper.

Serves 4

Moo Shu

1 tbsp (15 ml) toasted sesame oil

1 tsp grated ginger

1 tsp grated garlic

1 scallion, trimmed and minced

1 package Impossible™ meat

½ tsp five-spice powder

2 cups (140 g) mixed cabbage slaw

1 cup (210 g) sliced shiitake mushrooms

2 tbsp (30 ml) hoisin sauce

¼ cup (60 ml) soy sauce

2 tbsp (30 ml) mirin

1 tbsp (15 ml) oyster sauce

Sesame seeds, for garnish

Scallions, thinly sliced, for garnish

8 taco-sized flour tortillas

A popular Chinese restaurant dish usually made with pork or chicken and mandarin pancakes, moo shu easily adapts for use with alternative meats. Rather than spend time chopping up two kinds of cabbage, I use the precut slaw cabbage you find bagged in the supermarket produce section. While traditional moo shu calls for wood-ear mushrooms—and you can certainly use them if you like—I'm not a particular fan of their texture, so I substitute sliced shiitakes instead. Mandarin pancakes are the traditional accompaniment, but if you can't find them, taco-size Mexican flour tortillas work incredibly well.

Heat the sesame oil in a large frying pan or wok and add the ginger, garlic and scallion. Fry for 1 minute, then add the alternative meat, using a spoon to break it up.

Stir in the five-spice powder and mix well, cooking for 6 to 7 minutes, or until the alternative meat is nicely browned. Add the slaw and mushrooms and fry for 4 to 5 minutes, until they begin to soften.

Add the hoisin sauce, soy sauce, mirin and oyster sauce and mix very well. Pour the mixture into a bowl and garnish with sesame seeds and scallions.

To serve, place 1 to 2 tablespoons (15 to 30 g) of moo shu filling into a flour tortilla and eat like a taco.

Keema (Indian Ground "Meat" Curry with Tomatoes)

Serves 4

2 tsp (10 ml) safflower oil

1 small onion, minced

3 cloves garlic, minced

2 tsp (10 g) grated ginger

1 package Beyond Meat® or Impossible™ meat

2 tsp (3 g) garam masala

1 (15-oz [425-g]) can diced tomatoes

¼ cup (60 ml) water

1 cup (145 g) fresh or frozen green peas

2 tbsp (8 g) chopped fresh cilantro, for garnish

You can think of keema as an Indian-style chili that uses green sweet peas, fresh tomatoes and Indian spices, including garam masala, which is now available in the traditional spice aisle of most supermarkets. Serve keema with Chelo (page 121).

Heat the safflower oil in a large, deep frying pan over medium heat and add the onion. Fry for 5 to 6 minutes, or until the onion begins to soften and become translucent, then add the garlic and ginger. Fry for 1 minute more.

Add the alternative meat and use a wooden spoon to break it up. Fry for 6 to 7 minutes, or until the meat is browned. Stir in the garam masala and fry, stirring, for 1 minute.

Stir in the tomatoes with their liquid and the water and mix well. Simmer for 5 to 6 minutes, then add the peas. Cook for 5 minutes more.

Serve garnished with cilantro.

Chicken-Less Tikka Masala

For the turkey balls

2 (8-oz [226-g]) packages Trader Joe's® Turkeyless Protein Patties

1 tsp salt

½ tsp freshly ground black pepper

1 tsp garlic powder

2 tsp (3 g) garam masala

2 tbsp (30 ml) safflower oil

For the sauce

1 tbsp (14 g) vegan butter such as Earth Balance®

1 small onion, chopped

2 cloves garlic, grated

2 tsp (10 g) grated ginger

2 tbsp (32 g) tomato paste

2 tsp (3 g) garam masala

1 cup (240 ml) vegetable stock

1 cup (240 ml) coconut cream, stirred well

1 tbsp (11 g) dried fenugreek leaves (optional)

2 tbsp (8 g) chopped cilantro leaves, for garnish

This recipe uses Trader Joe's® Turkeyless Protein Patties that you'll form into the correct shape. I strongly encourage you to make the sauce ahead of time and allow it to sit at least overnight in the refrigerator. The reason is that without the long simmering time that is required to cook through actual meat, the flavors won't meld as well. Take this extra step; you'll be happy you did because the end result will be a more complex, richer-flavored sauce to buoy up the vegan meat pieces. Serve over Chelo (page 121) or with your favorite pita bread or naan.

Make the turkey balls: Mix the alternative meat in a large bowl with the salt, pepper, garlic powder and garam masala. Form into 1-inch (2.5-cm) balls, then slightly flatten into ovals and refrigerate until ready to use.

Make the sauce: Heat a deep saucepan over medium heat and add the butter. When the butter melts, add the onion and fry 6 to 7 minutes, or until it begins to soften and become translucent. Add the garlic and ginger and fry for 30 seconds, then add the tomato paste. Cook while stirring with a whisk for 1 minute.

Add the garam masala, cook for 30 seconds, then whisk in the vegetable stock. Add the coconut cream and whisk well, until the mixture is smooth. Simmer for 5 to 7 minutes. Remove from the heat and cool. Chill overnight.

Cook the turkey balls: Heat a skillet with the safflower oil over medium-low heat. Flatten each ball slightly into a more oval shape and add each to the pan. Do not crowd the pieces. Brown slightly on each side, 1 to 2 minutes per side, then remove and set aside.

Remove the sauce from the refrigerator and heat it in a medium pan over medium heat and bring to a simmer. Add the balls and simmer for 5 to 7 minutes more, or until the sauce is reduced by one-third and thickened.

Rub the fenugreek leaves, if using, together between your palms and add to the pot. Simmer for 1 minute. Garnish with cilantro leaves before serving.

CHAPTER 4

Tastes of Italy, the Middle East & Africa

Serves 4

Sausage & Peppers

1 tbsp (15 ml) olive oil

1 large onion, sliced

2 Italian green peppers or 1 green bell pepper, stemmed, seeded and sliced

1 red bell pepper, stemmed, seeded and sliced

1 package (400 g) Beyond Sausage® Sweet or Hot Italian

5 cloves garlic, sliced

½ tsp dried oregano

5 or 6 fresh basil leaves, torn

Growing up in New York City, I looked forward to the various Italian festivals around town, particularly for the delicious Italian sausages and peppers that were sold by street vendors. Tucked into a nice wedge of Italian bread so you could eat and walk, the sandwich was more than filling. You can serve these sausages and peppers with Italian bread as a sandwich or on a plate with cold pasta salad as a nice accompaniment.

Heat the olive oil in a large frying pan over medium heat and add the onion and green peppers. Reduce heat to medium-low and fry for 3 to 4 minutes.

Add the red bell pepper and fry this mixture for another 10 minutes. The onion should be softened and browned.

Push aside the onion and peppers in the pan and raise the heat to medium. Add the alternative sausage to the pan and fry for 6 minutes, turning halfway through the cooking time to brown on all sides.

Remove the sausage from the pan and slice each one diagonally into ½-inch (1.3-cm) slices. Set these aside.

Add the garlic to the pan and cook for 1 minute more. Stir in the oregano and return the sausage to the pan. Mix well and cook for 1 to 2 minutes more. Add the basil leaves and mix well. Serve hot.

Italian Wedding Soup

½ lb (227 g) Beyond Meat®

½ lb (227 g) Impossible™ meat

1 tsp onion powder

1 tsp garlic powder

½ tsp coarse salt

Freshly ground pepper to taste

1 tsp dried oregano

¼ cup (27 g) regular or gluten-free breadcrumbs

¼ cup (20 g) nutritional yeast or grated vegan Parmesan cheese such as Violife (optional)

2 tsp (10 ml) plus 1 tbsp (15 ml) olive oil, divided

1 rib celery, trimmed and minced

1 carrot, peeled, trimmed and minced

1 small onion, minced

3 cloves garlic, minced

1 quart (960 ml) vegetable stock

5 basil leaves

2 cups (60 g) fresh baby spinach or escarole, washed, trimmed and shredded

1 cup (112 g) cooked ditalini, small elbow or other small, cut pasta

This soup is so called not because it's served at weddings, but because of the "marriage" of all of the ingredients to create a hearty soup that is a meal in and of itself. It's important to let the finished soup sit so the flavors can balance. This is a great soup to make the day before and allow to sit in the refrigerator before reheating and serving with crusty bread.

Preheat the oven to 350°F (177°C). In a large bowl, mix together the alternative meats, onion and garlic powders, salt, black pepper and oregano. Mix very well with your hands to combine.

Mix in the breadcrumbs and nutritional yeast, if using, and mix well to combine. Form the mixture into 1-inch (2.5-cm) balls.

Pour 2 teaspoons (10 ml) of the olive oil into a baking dish and add the meatballs, turning over to coat. Bake for 10 minutes, or until lightly brown. Set aside.

Heat the remaining tablespoon (15 ml) of the oil in a large saucepan, then add the celery and carrot and fry for 5 minutes. Add the onion and fry for 4 to 5 minutes more. Stir in the garlic and fry for 1 minute.

Pour in the vegetable stock then add the basil and spinach and simmer for 5 to 6 minutes.

Stir in the ditalini and meatballs and simmer for 1 to 2 minutes. Cover and allow to sit so the flavors "marry" for 10 to 12 minutes.

Serves 4 to 6

Pasta Bolognese

1 tbsp (15 ml) olive oil

1 small onion, minced

1 carrot, peeled, trimmed and diced small

2 cloves garlic, minced

½ lb (227 g) Beyond Meat®

½ lb (227 g) Impossible™ meat

1 tbsp (16 g) tomato paste

1 (14-oz [400-g]) can diced tomatoes

1 bay leaf

Salt to taste

Freshly ground pepper to taste

½ cup (120 ml) unsweetened almond milk

1 lb (454 g) cooked pappardelle

¼ cup (25 g) grated Violife or other alternative Parmesan cheese or more as needed

Bolognese sauce is traditionally made with ground beef or a combination of ground beef and pork. Here we are using a mixture of Beyond Meat® and Impossible™ meat. Milk rather than cream is what makes a classic Bolognese, but in this recipe, we will be using almond milk to keep it vegan. For the best result, chop the carrot and onion finely enough so they are roughly the same size as the ground "meat" crumbles. Serve it over pappardelle—the wide egg-based noodle.

Heat the olive oil in a large, deep sauté pan over medium heat. Add the onion and carrot and sauté for 5 to 6 minutes. Add the garlic and sauté for 1 minute more.

Add the alternative meats and break them up into crumbles using a wooden spoon. Fry for 6 to 7 minutes, or until beginning to brown, stirring often.

Add the tomato paste and stir well. Cook for 1 minute and add the tomatoes, bay leaf, salt and pepper. Mix well, reduce heat to medium-low and simmer for 10 minutes. Add the milk and mix well. Simmer for another 10 minutes.

Make sure to remove the bay leaf before serving. Serve spooned over cooked pappardelle and topped with cheese.

Classic Italian Meatballs

½ lb (227 g) Beyond Meat®

½ lb (227 g) Impossible™ meat

1 tsp onion powder

1 tsp garlic powder

½ tsp coarse salt

Freshly ground pepper to taste

1 tsp dried oregano

¼ cup (27 g) regular or gluten-free breadcrumbs

¼ cup (20 g) nutritional yeast or grated vegan Parmesan cheese such as Violife (optional)

2 tsp (10 ml) olive oil

1 pint (480 ml) jarred marinara sauce of your choice

These meatballs in pomodoro sauce are the natural pairing for spaghetti, but they are also excellent on a hero or sub roll. Add grated vegan Parmesan or mozzarella shreds to make a meatball parmigiana hero. As in all good Italian ground meat recipes, a mix of "beef" and "pork" gives a more well-rounded flavor. If you prefer one over the other, you don't have to mix the two. Serve these meatballs with spaghetti or on Italian bread as a sandwich.

Preheat the oven to 350°F (177°C). In a large bowl, mix together the alternative meats, onion and garlic powders, salt, pepper and oregano. Mix very well with your hands to combine.

Mix in the breadcrumbs and nutritional yeast, if using, and mix well to combine. Form the mixture into 3-inch (7.5-cm) balls. You should have about nine.

Pour the olive oil into a baking dish and add the meatballs, turning over to coat. Bake for 10 minutes, or until lightly brown.

Once cooked, add to your favorite marinara sauce and simmer for 5 to 6 minutes before serving.

Classic Italian Tomato Meat Sauce

Serves 4 to 6 over pasta

2 tsp (10 ml) olive oil

½ large carrot, peeled and minced

1 small onion, chopped small

3 cloves garlic, minced

1 package Beyond Meat® or Impossible™ meat

½ tsp coarse salt

Freshly ground pepper to taste

1 tsp dried oregano

4 cups (960 ml) plain tomato sauce

5 to 6 basil leaves, torn

Meat sauce is a classic and hearty topping for pasta, especially spaghetti. It's a great replacement for meatballs that allows you to have a bit of meat goodness in every forkful. Most importantly, plant-based meat mimics the "mouth feel" of ground meat that gives texture and robustness to a classic meat sauce.

Heat the olive oil in a large sauté pan over medium heat and add the carrot and onion. Fry for 6 to 7 minutes, or until the onion begins to soften and become translucent, then add the garlic and fry for 1 minute more.

Add the alternative meat and, using a wooden spoon to break up the chunks, fry for 4 minutes. Add the salt, pepper and oregano and mix well. Continue to fry, until browned and cooked through, 2 to 3 minutes longer.

Add the tomato sauce and basil leaves and mix well. Lower heat to a simmer and cook until the mixture is reduced by one-quarter, about 5 minutes.

Better-than-the-Real-Thing Lasagna

Serves 6

2 tsp (10 ml) olive oil

½ large carrot, peeled and minced

1 small onion, minced

3 cloves garlic, minced

1 package Beyond Meat® or Impossible™ meat

½ tsp coarse salt

Freshly ground pepper to taste

1 tsp dried oregano

4½ cups (1.1 L) jarred marinara sauce of your choice, divided

5 to 6 basil leaves, torn

1 box (255 g) no-boil lasagna noodles (you may use gluten-free)

1 cup (112 g) each vegan mozzarella, provolone and cheddar cheese, shredded and mixed together

5 slices vegan provolone

1 cup (100 g) grated vegan Parmesan cheese such as Violife, plus extra for topping

Vegan pesto (optional)

Few dishes have universally earned the "comfort food" label more than lasagna. It's great for a Sunday supper or a special occasion meal, and in some parts of the United States, it often makes an appearance on Thanksgiving tables alongside the turkey. You'll find your guests will be hard-pressed to realize this lasagna is vegan because it's equally as good—if not better!—than the real thing. Because cheese is so integral to lasagna, I've added a hefty amount. Reduce (or add more!) as you desire.

Preheat the oven to 350°F (177°C).

Heat the olive oil in a large sauté pan over medium heat and add the carrot and onion. Fry for 5 to 6 minutes, or until the onion begins to soften and become translucent, then add the garlic and fry for 1 minute more. Add the alternative meat and, using a wooden spoon to break up the chunks, fry for 4 minutes. Add the salt, pepper and oregano and mix well. Continue to fry until browned and cooked through, 4 to 5 minutes longer.

Add 2 cups (480 ml) of the marinara sauce and basil leaves and mix well. Lower heat to a simmer and cook until the mixture is reduced by one-quarter, about 5 minutes. Set aside.

Add ¼ cup (60 ml) of the remaining marinara sauce to the bottom of an 8 x 8–inch (20 x 20–cm) baking pan and layer in 3 lasagna noodles. They may overlap. Spread one-quarter of the meat mixture onto the noodles and top with one-quarter of the remaining marinara sauce and cheese mixture. Add another layer of noodles on top and repeat until all the meat filling and cheese are used up. Finish with a layer of noodles and top this with about ¼ cup (60 ml) of marinara sauce, the provolone slices and Parmesan cheese.

Drizzle with pesto, if desired, and cover with tinfoil and bake for 15 to 20 minutes. Remove from the oven and cool for 5 minutes. Serve hot.

Kebabs Four Ways

Ground meat kebabs are popular in a variety of cultures, where they are often served as street food. While normally cooked on a grill, over an open fire or in a clay oven, these kebab variations are easily cooked in a home oven. They are great for summer grilling, but if you cook them this way, start them off on the grill on a piece of tinfoil. Cook them for 2 to 3 minutes, until they firm up, before turning them over onto the grill itself.

Moroccan Kebabs

Makes 6 kebabs

For the kebabs

1 package Beyond Meat® or Impossible™ meat

1 small onion, grated

1 clove garlic, grated

2 tsp (5 g) Ras el Hanout (page 115)

1 tsp salt

¼ cup (27 g) regular or gluten-free breadcrumbs

½ cup (30 g) chopped fresh cilantro

For the vegetables

2 tsp (10 ml) olive oil

4 plum tomatoes, sliced into quarters

1 small onion, sliced into wedges

Chermoula (page 116), for serving

Ras el hanout, or "top of the shop," is a Moroccan spice mix that is essential to these kebabs. Ras el hanout is also excellent on roasted or grilled vegetables. You can find it at gourmet grocers, Middle Eastern markets and online, but it's easy enough to make and store yourself with the recipe on page 115. Kalustyan's in Manhattan is an excellent source as well. Serve these with pita bread or couscous.

Preheat the oven to 350°F (177°C).

Make the kebabs: In a large bowl, combine all the ingredients for the kebabs. Mix well with a rubber spatula or knead using your hands. Divide the mixture into 6 equal-sized balls and refrigerate, covered in plastic, for 30 minutes.

Shape the kebabs: Form into a rectangle, approximately 8 inches (20 cm) long and 2 inches (5 cm) wide. You may do this on a sheet of tinfoil that is 14 inches (36 cm) long and folded in half like a book. Spray the tinfoil with cooking spray and place one portion of the mixture on one side of the tinfoil and fold the other side of foil over it. Flatten the mixture through the foil with the palm of your hand and smooth in both directions until the mixture is about ⅛ inch (3 mm) thick. Open the foil and fold the flattened "meat" mixture over itself, fold over the foil and smooth again. Open the foil and fold up each of the kebabs' short edges slightly to square it off. Repeat with each portion.

Cook the kebabs and the vegetables: Place each finished kebab on a cookie sheet or baking tray lined with tinfoil that has been sprayed with cooking spray or brushed with 1 teaspoon of safflower oil. Toss the olive oil, tomatoes and onion together in a bowl and arrange around the kebabs. Bake for 10 to 15 minutes, or until golden brown. If grilling, you may place the kebabs onto tinfoil and after they are "set"—2 to 3 minutes into the cooking process—you can turn them over onto the hot grill for 5 to 6 minutes more.

Remove the kebabs from the oven and arrange on a platter with the tomatoes and onion. Drizzle the kebabs with Chermoula and serve.

Makes about ½ cup (48 g)

Ras el Hanout

1 tsp ground cumin

1 tsp ground ginger

1 tsp coarse salt

1 tsp freshly ground black pepper

½ tsp ground cinnamon

¼ tsp ginger

¼ tsp nutmeg

¼ tsp cardamom

½ tsp ground coriander

½ tsp cayenne pepper

½ tsp ground allspice

¼ tsp ground cloves

Variations of this spice mixture are used in North Africa and can differ from household to household and region to region. Use it on grilled vegetables, alternative meat kebabs, vegan hamburgers and in stews. I encourage you to experiment with a version you like best. All of the spices are easily found in any supermarket spice aisle. The recipe can be scaled up. It will keep, properly stored, for up to three months.

Combine all of the ingredients in a bowl, whisking to combine.

Store in an airtight glass jar in a cool, dark place.

Makes about 1 cup (240 ml)

Chermoula

4 cloves garlic, finely chopped

1 bunch cilantro, washed well and patted or spun dry

2 tbsp (30 ml) fresh lemon juice

2 tsp (5 g) paprika

1 tsp ground cumin

1 tsp salt

¼ cup (21 g) cayenne pepper

⅛ tsp powdered saffron

¼ cup (60 ml) good-quality extra-virgin olive oil

Chermoula is an herbaceous sauce with an olive oil base that is delicious for dipping breads or for drizzling on top of kebabs or grilled vegetables.

Combine all the ingredients, except the olive oil, in the bowl of a food processor and process to a coarse paste. Slowly drizzle in the olive oil while processing, until you have a smooth sauce.

Store in an airtight container in the refrigerator for up to 3 days.

Lebanese Kofta Kebabs with Tahini Sauce

Makes 6 kebabs

For the kebabs

1 cup (60 g) packed parsley, leaves and stems removed

1 tbsp (7 g) regular or gluten-free breadcrumbs

1 small yellow onion, quartered

2 cloves garlic, whole

½ tsp salt

½ tsp freshly ground black pepper

½ tsp ground cumin

¼ tsp ground coriander

¼ tsp allspice

½ tsp sumac

⅛ tsp nutmeg

½ tsp pimenton

1 package Beyond Meat®

2 plum tomatoes, cored and cut into 4 large quarters

For the tahini sauce

3 cloves garlic, grated

Juice of 2 lemons

¼ cup (60 ml) tahini

½ tsp coarse salt

¼ cup (60 ml) ice water or more as needed

Pita bread, for serving (optional)

This recipe is inspired by Middle Eastern lamb kebabs called "kofta" that are usually eaten tucked into pita bread along with lettuce and tomato and generously drizzled with tahini sauce. I chose Beyond Meat® for this preparation because, like the animal meats traditionally used for this kebab, it is fattier. For the same reason, it's important to chill the Beyond Meat® mixture after mixing but before combining into the kebabs so they hold together on the grill.

Make the kebabs: Place the parsley leaves in a food processor along with the breadcrumbs and process for 30 seconds, until the leaves are finely ground. Add the onion, garlic, salt, pepper, cumin, coriander, allspice, sumac, nutmeg and pimenton and process into a smooth paste. Add the alternative meat and pulse a few times until completely combined. Scrape the mixture into a bowl and use a rubber spatula to mix more thoroughly if necessary. Divide the alternative meat mixture into 6 equal-size balls and refrigerate, covered in plastic, for about 30 minutes.

Shape the kebabs: Lightly spray a sheet of tinfoil with cooking spray and place on a cookie sheet or sheet pan. Form each ball into a log that is about 6 inches (15 cm) long and 1 inch (2.5 cm) thick. Place each log on the sprayed tinfoil about 1½ inches (4 cm) apart. Using your forefinger, gently press indentations down the length of each kebab at regular intervals.

Preheat a grill on high or heat the oven on the broil setting. Place the tomatoes on the tinfoil or on a kebab skewer. Grill or broil the kebabs for 6 to 7 minutes, or until golden brown, flipping them over using a spatula about halfway through the cooking time. If grilling, you may place the kebabs onto tinfoil and after they are "set"—2 to 3 minutes into cooking—you can turn them over on the hot grill for 5 to 6 minutes more. Grill or broil the tomatoes until the skin is well-charred.

Make the sauce: Mix the garlic and lemon juice and set aside for 15 minutes. Combine the lemon juice mixture, tahini and salt in a blender or small food processor along with 2 tablespoons (30 ml) of the water. Process until the ingredients are combined and thick. Slowly add more water while processing the mixture until you have a smooth sauce. Serve kebabs hot with the tomatoes on the side along with pita bread, if desired, and 1 to 2 tablespoons (15 to 30 ml) of tahini sauce.

Serves 4

Persian Kebabs

For the kebabs

1 small onion, grated

1 clove garlic, grated

1 tsp onion powder

¼ tsp garlic powder

½ tsp ground cumin

½ tsp turmeric powder

1 tsp pimenton

1 tsp salt

½ tsp freshly ground black pepper

¼ cup (27 g) regular or gluten-free breadcrumbs

1 lb (454 g) Beyond Meat®

4 plum tomatoes, sliced into quarters

For the sauce

½ stick or 4 tbsp (56 g) vegan butter

½ tsp powdered saffron, crushed and dissolved in ¼ cup (60 ml) boiling water

Kabob koobideh is the Persian version of a ground meat kebab. Flavored with grated onion, garlic and spices, the kebabs are usually made from a combination of lamb and beef and normally formed around a flat skewer called a seekh. In this version, tinfoil is used to fold and smooth the mixture into long rectangles to approximate the shape. Use Beyond Meat® for this because of its higher fat content—an important aspect to forming these kebabs and creating a juicy flavor. These kebabs are cooked over a wood fire in a tandoor, or clay-lined oven, and this recipe calls for pimenton to impart the smoky flavor that would normally come from the wood fire.

Preheat the oven to 350°F (177°C).

Make the kebabs: In a large bowl, combine all the ingredients for the kebabs, except the tomatoes. Mix well with a rubber spatula or knead well with your hands. Divide the mixture into 6 equal-sized balls and refrigerate, covered in plastic, for 80 minutes.

Shape the kebabs: Form into a rectangle, approximately 8 inches (20 cm) long and 2 inches (5 cm) wide. You may do this on a sheet of tinfoil that is 14 inches (36 cm) long and folded in half like a book. Spray the tinfoil with cooking spray and place one portion of the mixture on one side of the tinfoil and fold the other side of foil over it. Flatten the mixture through the foil with the palm of your hand and smooth in both directions, until the mixture is about ⅛ inch (3 mm) thick. Open the foil and fold the flattened "meat" mixture over itself, fold over the foil and smooth again. Open the foil and fold up each of the kebabs' short edges slightly to square it off. Repeat with each portion.

Cook the kebabs: Place each finished kebab on a cookie sheet or baking tray lined with tinfoil that has been sprayed with cooking spray or brushed with 1 teaspoon of safflower oil. Arrange the tomatoes around the kebabs. Bake for 10 to 15 minutes, or until golden brown. If grilling, you may place the kebabs onto tinfoil and after they are "set"—2 to 3 minutes into the cooking—you can turn them over onto the hot grill for 5 to 6 minutes more.

While the kebabs are cooking, make the sauce: Melt the butter in a small saucepan and add the saffron-infused water.

Remove the kebabs from the oven and arrange on a platter with the tomatoes. Pour the saffron butter sauce over the finished kebabs.

Serve with Chelo (page 121).

Chelo (Persian Steamed White Rice)

Serves 4 to 6

2 cups (392 g) high-quality aged Dehraduni basmati rice such as Lal Quila

1 tbsp (18 g) coarse salt

1 tbsp (15 ml) plus ¼ cup (60 ml) olive oil, divided

The secret to the long, fluffy grains of Persian rice is steaming the rice in a pan covered with a clean dish towel that wicks the excess moisture away from the rice as it steams. Soaking the rice for at least one hour and up to overnight is recommended to ensure the longest possible grains as the rice absorbs the water and expands. Soaking also shortens the cooking time considerably. Although this is a traditional step, you can certainly make rice without soaking it—and for everyday meals, I often do.

A prized aspect of chelo is tahdig, the crispy crust of rice at the bottom of the pan. Made correctly, the tahdig should come out in one piece and be placed on the table alongside the rice for everyone to share a little piece.

Wash the rice by placing it in a deep bowl and filling it with cold water. Swirl the water around with your hand until it is cloudy. Carefully drain the water. Repeat four or five times, until the water is clear. Set aside.

Bring 6 cups (1.4 L) of water to a boil in a large, nonstick saucepot or a large iron pot and add the salt and 1 tablespoon (15 ml) of the oil.

Add the rice and simmer on medium-low for 10 to 15 minutes. Drain in a colander.

Add ¼ cup (60 ml) of water and 1 tablespoon (15 ml) of the oil to the rice pot. Swirl it around. Add 1 large spoonful of rice into the middle of the pot and add spoonful after spoonful in a mound, until all the rice is used.

Drizzle the remaining oil over the rice and pour another ¼ cup (60 ml) of water over it. Use a rubber spatula to smooth the pyramid up into a cone.

Place a clean dish towel or doubled-up paper towels over the pot and then squeeze the lid into place. Place over low heat for 20 to 25 minutes.

Remove the rice and place it on a platter. To remove the tahdig, or rice crust, take the pot and carefully hold the bottom under cold water. Then, use the spatula to loosen the crust. Turn it out onto a platter.

Makes 6 kebabs

Indian-Style Seekh Kebabs

2 small onions, divided (1 quartered and 1 cut into wedges)

2 cloves garlic, quartered

2 tsp (10 g) grated ginger

1 green chili, stemmed and seeded

½ cup (46 g) fresh mint leaves

½ cup (32 g) fresh cilantro leaves

1 tsp salt

1 package Beyond Meat® or Impossible™ meat

½ tsp ground coriander

½ tsp ground cumin

3 tsp (15 ml) safflower oil, plus more as needed

These kebabs are so named because of the long, flat skewers used to make them, called seekhs, which are then cooked in a tandoor clay oven. You can approximate the same shape by simply molding the kebabs into the shape with your hands or using a method (described in the recipe) to fold it into shape using tinfoil. Serve this dish with Chelo (page 121), or with pita bread or a salad.

Preheat the oven to 350°F (177°C).

Make the kebabs: In a large bowl, combine the quartered onion, garlic, ginger, chili, mint, cilantro and salt in the bowl of a food processor or in a high-powered blender and process into a paste.

Scrape the herb paste into a bowl along with the alternative meat, coriander and cumin. Mix well with a rubber spatula or knead using your hands. Divide the mixture into 6 equal-size balls and refrigerate, covered in plastic, for 30 minutes.

Shape the kebabs: Form into a rectangle, approximately 8 inches (20 cm) long and 2 inches (5 cm) wide. You may do this on a sheet of tinfoil that is 14 inches (36 cm) long and folded in half like a book. Spray the tinfoil with cooking spray and place one portion of the mixture on one side of the tinfoil and fold the other side of foil over it. Flatten the mixture through the foil with the palm of your hand and smooth in both directions, until the mixture is about ⅛ inch (3 mm) thick. Open the foil and fold the flattened "meat" mixture over itself, fold over the foil and smooth again. Open the foil and fold up each of the kebabs' short edges slightly to square it off. Repeat with each portion.

Cook the kebabs: Place each finished kebab on a cookie sheet or baking tray lined with tinfoil that has been sprayed with cooking spray or brushed with 1 teaspoon of safflower oil. Toss the onion wedges together in a bowl with an additional teaspoon of oil and arrange around the kebabs. Drizzle the kebabs with more oil and bake for 15 to 20 minutes, or until golden brown. If grilling, you may place the kebabs onto tinfoil and after they are "set"—2 to 3 minutes into cooking—you can turn them over onto the hot grill for 5 to 6 minutes more.

Remove the kebabs from the oven and arrange on a platter with the onion.

Serves 4 to 6

Khoresht Geimeh (Persian Lentil Potato Stew)

....

For the meatballs

1 lb (454 g) Beyond Meat® or Impossible™ meat

1 tsp onion powder

1 tsp garlic powder

½ tsp ground cumin

½ tsp turmeric powder

¼ tsp black pepper

½ tsp kosher salt

For the stew

1 cup (200 g) yellow split peas

2 tbsp (30 ml) olive oil

1 medium onion, thinly sliced

1 clove garlic, thinly sliced

1 tsp salt

1 tsp freshly ground black pepper

1 tsp turmeric powder

½ tsp cinnamon

1 tbsp (16 g) tomato paste

4 cups (960 ml) vegetable stock

½ tsp powdered saffron, crushed and dissolved in ¼ cup (60 ml) boiling water

1 dried Persian lime or ¼ cup (60 ml) fresh lime juice

½ cup (120 ml) grapeseed oil

2 large Yukon Gold potatoes or 1 large Russet potato, peeled and julienned

Chelo (page 121)

Khoresht Geimeh is a classic Persian stew and a little bit is often served as a garnishment on top of tahdig. (See the Chelo recipe on page 121.) Khoresht Geimeh is a study in textures: The soft bite of the lentils is a counterpoint to crispy french-fried potatoes. I've even known a cook or two who have used packaged fried potato sticks—found in the potato chip aisle—for the crispiest effect. I find that Yukon gold or Russet potatoes are best for french fries that hold their shape.

Make the meatballs: Combine all the ingredients and form into meatballs about 1 inch (2.5 cm) in diameter. Place on a cookie sheet or baking dish. Broil for 7 to 8 minutes, or until lightly brown. Set aside.

Make the stew: Boil the split peas on medium-low heat in 1 cup (240 ml) of water for 10 minutes, or until just cooked around the edges. Skim the foam from the pot while cooking, as needed. Drain the peas and rinse them in a colander. Set aside.

Heat the olive oil in a large, heavy saucepan over medium heat. Add the onion and cook until they begin to soften and become translucent, 4 to 5 minutes. Add the garlic and cook for about 1 minute more.

Add the salt, pepper, turmeric and cinnamon. Stir well and cook for 1 minute more. Mix in the tomato paste and stir well. Cook for 30 to 40 seconds. Add the vegetable stock and the saffron-infused water.

Poke a little hole in the dried lime, if using, with a sharp knife and add it to the pot. Otherwise, add the lime juice. Allow to simmer on medium-low for 10 minutes, then stir in the yellow split peas and cook for 15 minutes more.

While the stew is simmering, make the fried potatoes. Heat the oil in a large, shallow sauté pan on medium heat and add the potatoes. Sauté until golden brown, then remove with a slotted spoon. Drain on paper towels or on a wire rack set over a sheet tray.

Serve the stew garnished with the fried potato sticks and Chelo.

Kufteh (Middle Eastern Rice Meatballs)

Serves 4

For the meatballs

1 tbsp (15 ml) olive oil

1 small onion, minced

2 cloves garlic, minced

1 package Beyond Meat® or Impossible™ meat

1 tsp turmeric powder

½ tsp cinnamon

1 tsp salt

Freshly ground black pepper to taste

1 tbsp (16 g) tomato paste

2 cups (372 g) cooked basmati rice

½ cup (90 g) cooked yellow split peas

2 tbsp (11 g) minced fresh mint

2 tbsp (8 g) minced fresh tarragon

2 tbsp (7 g) minced fresh dill

2 tbsp (8 g) minced fresh parsley

¼ cup (60 ml) vegan liquid egg substitute

1 tbsp (8 g) rice flour

8 seedless sour Persian plums or pitted prunes

For the sauce

1 tbsp (15 ml) olive oil

1 tbsp (16 g) tomato paste

1 cup (252 g) pureed tomato

1 cup (240 ml) sour plum juice

2 tsp (9 g) sugar

½ tsp onion powder

½ tsp cinnamon

These wonderful meatballs are more like a self-contained meal in and of themselves. Kufteh means "mashed" and refers to the way the ingredients are smashed together to form meatballs. The sauce is made from sour plum juice, which can be found in Middle Eastern markets. If you can't find it, you can substitute 1 cup (240 ml) of pomegranate juice and 2 teaspoons (9 g) of sugar.

Make the meatballs: Heat the olive oil in a large frying pan over medium heat and add the onion. Cook for 4 to 5 minutes, or until the onion begins to soften and become translucent. Add the garlic and cook for 1 minute more.

Add the alternative meat, using a wooden spoon to break up the chunks. Fry for 6 to 7 minutes, or until browned. Stir in the turmeric, cinnamon, salt and pepper. Add the tomato paste and stir well. Cook for 1 minute more.

Scrape the meat mixture into a large bowl and add the rice, peas, mint, tarragon, dill and parsley. Mix very well and add the egg substitute. Add the flour and mix well. You should be able to make a ball that holds together from the mixture. Make 8 equal-sized meatballs and push a sour plum or prune into the center, reforming the meatball around it. Set aside in the refrigerator for 30 minutes.

Make the sauce: Heat the olive oil in a large, deep saucepan and add the tomato paste. Cook for 1 to 2 minutes then add the pureed tomato and mix well. Cook for 3 to 5 minutes, then add the sour plum juice. Add the sugar, onion powder and cinnamon and bring to a simmer for 5 minutes.

Place the formed kufteh in the pot with the sauce and simmer, uncovered, for 5 to 7 minutes more.

Serve the meatballs in a bowl with the sauce.

Persian Kotlet
(Potato & Ground "Meat" Patties)

Serves 4

2 lbs (906 g) Yukon gold potatoes, grated

1 medium yellow onion, sliced in half

1 clove garlic, minced

½ lb (227 g) Beyond Meat® or Impossible™ meat

1 tsp turmeric powder

⅓ tsp ground cumin

1 tsp coarse salt

½ tsp freshly ground black pepper

⅓ cup (80 ml) safflower oil

I like to make kotlet and keep them on hand—they keep a few days in the refrigerator—for picnics, a simple snack or a fast lunch. Consider wrapping them in flat bread or tucking them into a pita with a shmear of hummus or tahini sauce (page 118). I also like to eat them with a slice of avocado, crisp lettuce or a slice of ripe tomato. The grater attachment on a food processor makes short work of grating the potato, but any hand grater will do nicely as well.

Place about one-quarter of the shredded potatoes in a clean (non-terry) kitchen towel and fold the sides of the towel to completely envelop the potatoes. Wring the towel as hard as you can to squeeze out any water. Place the wrung-out potatoes in a bowl and set aside. Repeat until all the potato is used.

Place the potatoes in the bowl of a food processor outfitted with the metal blade and add the onion and garlic. Pulse until the ingredients are smooth but not watery, about 15 seconds. If you do not have a food processor, you may simply grate the onion and garlic by hand and add it to the grated potatoes in the bowl.

Scrape the mixture out of the food processor bowl into a large bowl and add the alternative meat. Add the turmeric, cumin, salt and pepper. Using your hands, knead the mixture lightly until all the ingredients are incorporated and it is even in color.

Heat a large nonstick or cast-iron skillet over medium heat and add the safflower oil. Wet your hands lightly and take a lemon-size amount of the kotlet mixture out of the bowl and roll it into an egg shape. Flatten gently and press it out so you have a patty that is about ¼ inch (6 mm) thick. Gently place the patty into the skillet. Repeat until the skillet is filled but not crowded.

Fry the patties until lightly browned, about 5 minutes, then flip over and fry another 5 minutes. While the patties are frying, preheat the oven to 350°F (177°C) and prepare a sheet pan with tinfoil.

Once the patties are browned, remove them from the pan and place on a wire rack or directly onto the sheet tray. Bake in the oven for 10 minutes. This ensures the kotlet are cooked through but not too greasy.

Serve kotlet warm or cold, plain or with tahini sauce.

Moussaka

For the eggplant

1 medium eggplant, stemmed, peeled and cut lengthwise into ¼-inch (6-mm) slices

Coarse salt as needed

2 tbsp (30 ml) good-quality olive oil

For the meat mixture

1 tbsp (15 ml) olive oil

1 small onion, minced

4 cloves garlic, minced

1 package Beyond Meat® or Impossible™ meat

1 tsp salt

1 tsp freshly ground black pepper

1 tsp cinnamon

2 tsp (5 g) paprika

1 tbsp (16 g) tomato paste

½ cup (120 ml) dry white wine

1 (15-oz [425-g]) can crushed tomatoes

1 tbsp (6 g) minced fresh mint

1 tbsp (4 g) minced fresh parsley

For the béchamel

3 tbsp (42 g) vegan butter

2 tbsp (16 g) flour

2 cups (480 ml) dairy-free milk

Pinch of nutmeg

½ tsp salt

Freshly ground black pepper to taste

1 cup (113 g) shredded vegan provolone cheese

1 tsp nutritional yeast

Paprika as needed

Moussaka is a Greek casserole that features ground meat, thinly sliced browned eggplant and a béchamel sauce. It is excellent the day it's made or as leftovers the day after. It's important to salt your eggplant slices as a way to leech out the bitterness. This can be done up to one hour before cooking.

Preheat the oven to 350°F (177°C).

Make the eggplant: Place the eggplant slices in a single layer on a cookie sheet and salt both sides generously. Set aside for 10 to 15 minutes and up to 60 minutes. Rinse off the brown liquid that will leech from the eggplant slices and pat dry with a paper towel.

Heat a large frying pan with the olive oil over medium heat, then add the eggplant slices and fry for 2 to 3 minutes per side, until golden brown. Remove from the pan and place on a wire rack set over a cookie sheet or onto a plate lined with paper towels. Set aside.

Make the meat mixture: Heat the olive oil in a large, heavy saucepan over medium heat. Add the onion and cook until it begins to soften and become translucent, 4 to 5 minutes. Add the garlic and cook for about 1 minute more.

Add the alternative meat and use a wooden spoon to break up the chunks. Fry for 6 to 7 minutes, or until browned. Add the salt, pepper, cinnamon and paprika. Stir well and cook for 1 minute more. Mix in the tomato paste and stir well. Cook for 30 to 40 seconds. Add the wine, stir and cook for 40 to 60 seconds, or until the wine evaporates. Stir in the tomatoes, mint and parsley and simmer for 5 to 7 minutes, then set aside.

Make the béchamel: Heat the butter in a medium saucepan over medium-low heat, until it melts. Stir in the flour, and using a whisk, mix well. Cook, stirring, for 1 to 2 minutes. Slowly add the milk, stirring the whole time. Add the nutmeg, salt and pepper and simmer for 3 to 4 minutes, or until the mixture thickens enough to just coat the back of a spoon. Remove the béchamel from the heat and stir in the cheese and nutritional yeast, whisking until the cheese melts.

Assemble the moussaka: Pour the alternative meat mixture into an 8 x 8–inch (20 x 20–cm) baking dish and layer the eggplant on top. Spread the béchamel mixture on top of the eggplant and shake the pan to ensure the sauce is distributed evenly. Sprinkle the top of the sauce with paprika.

Bake the moussaka for 10 to 15 minutes, or until the top is bubbling and light brown. Cool slightly and serve.

Loobia Polow
(Persian Green Bean Rice Pilaf)

Serves 4 to 6

1½ tbsp (21 ml) olive oil, divided

½ lb (227 g) green beans, trimmed and cut into 1-inch (2.5-cm) pieces

1 medium onion, thinly sliced

1 clove garlic, thinly sliced

1 lb (454 g) Beyond Meat® or Impossible™ meat

2 tsp (12 g) salt, divided

¼ tsp black pepper

½ tsp ground cumin

½ tsp turmeric powder

½ tsp cinnamon

1 tbsp (16 g) tomato paste

1½ cups (360 ml) vegetable stock

½ tsp powdered saffron, crushed and dissolved in ¼ cup (60 ml) boiling water

2 tbsp (30 ml) fresh lemon juice

1 tsp sugar

1 cup (196 g) basmati rice

Polow is a general term for a variety of Persian layered rice dishes comprising small amounts of meat and abundant vegetables. Polow is the precursor to "pilafs" in the European tradition and is considered one of the iconic hallmarks of Persian cuisine. Biryani—the Indian version of polow—was created when Mughal emperors of 16th-century India adopted Persian cooking styles into their royal courts after conquering Iran. These dishes are named after their vegetable component—loobia—which, in Farsi, means "green bean."

Heat 1 tablespoon (15 ml) of the olive oil in a large frying pan and add the green beans and onion. Fry until the onion begins to soften and become translucent, 6 to 7 minutes. Add the garlic and cook for about 1 minute more.

Add the alternative meat and break it up with a wooden spoon. Fry for 6 to 7 minutes, or until browned on all sides. Add 1 teaspoon of the salt and the pepper, cumin, turmeric and cinnamon. Stir well and cook for 1 minute more. Mix in the tomato paste and stir well. Cook for 30 to 40 seconds. Add the vegetable stock and the saffron-infused water. Add the lemon juice and sugar and allow to simmer on medium-low for 10 minutes.

Wash the rice: Place the rice in a large, deep bowl and add enough cold water to cover. Swirl the rice around with your hand until the water is cloudy and then gently pour it out, making sure not to spill out any rice. Repeat four to five times or until the water is mostly clear.

Bring the rice and 2 cups (480 ml) of water to a boil in a large, deep pot, preferably nonstick. Add the remaining salt and olive oil. Reduce heat to medium and cook the rice for 12 minutes, stirring once or twice. Drain.

Pour ¼ cup (60 ml) of water into the same pot in which you boiled the rice. Using a large spoon or spatula, spoon one-quarter of the rice into the middle of the pot. Add one-third of the green bean mixture on top of the rice and then another one-quarter of the rice. Continue until all the rice and green bean mixture is used, finishing with the rice on top. You should have a "pyramid," or mound, in the middle of the pot. Cover the pot with a clean dish towel or a doubled-up paper towel and then firmly press the pot lid on top. Fold up the edges of the towel over the top of the lid so it is not near the fire. Cook on the lowest heat setting for 15 minutes.

Spoon the rice onto a platter to serve.

Jollof Rice

Serves 4 to 6

1 tbsp (15 ml) safflower oil

1 small onion, chopped

3 cloves garlic, grated

1 tsp grated ginger

½ scotch bonnet pepper, stemmed, seeded and minced

1 package Beyond Meat® or Impossible™ meat

2 tsp (5 g) Caribbean-style curry powder

1 tbsp (4 g) minced parsley

1 tsp minced thyme

1 tbsp (16 g) tomato paste

1 cup (250 g) crushed tomatoes

1 cup (196 g) basmati rice

1 cup (240 ml) vegetable stock

1 tsp salt

1 tbsp (14 g) vegan butter

Jollof rice is a West African one-pot dish that may or may not contain meat. Normally, the rice and meat cook together for an extended time, but here we are parcooking the rice to hasten the process. You can make this dish as spicy as you like with the addition of more or less scotch bonnet pepper.

Heat the safflower oil in a large, deep pot over medium heat and add the onion. Fry for 6 to 7 minutes, or until the onion begins to soften and become translucent. Add the garlic, ginger and pepper and fry for 1 to 2 minutes more. Do not allow the garlic to turn brown.

Add the alternative meat and use a wooden spoon to break it up. Fry for 6 to 7 minutes, until browned. Stir the curry powder, parsley and thyme into the meat and mix well. Fry for 1 minute more, then add the tomato paste and mix well. Stir in the tomatoes and reduce heat to a simmer.

Wash the rice by placing it in a deep bowl and filling it with cold water. Swirl the water around with your hand until it is cloudy. Carefully drain the water. Repeat four or five times, until the water is clear. Set aside.

Add the washed rice to the pan with the meat mixture. Stir in the vegetable stock and salt and stir well. Reduce heat to a simmer and cook, uncovered, for 20 minutes, or until the liquid is absorbed. Mix in the butter and then spoon the rice onto a platter to serve.

Acknowledgments

This book would not have been written if it weren't for a spark of an idea by my editor Marissa Giambelluca, who realized from a passing comment of mine about an alternative meat dish I had recently made, that there was definitely the need for a book like this for everyone out there interested in vegan eating.

Special thanks go to my family and friends, who were game taste-testers for these recipes—even when skeptical. I'm happy to say they all avowedly converted to alternative meats.

I'm most grateful for the generations of cooks across the world who have been creative enough to use ground meat in so many different ways—they provided the foundations for building an entire cookbook around alternative ground meat products.

And the most special thanks goes to my friend Victoria Kann, whose love for good food and her vegan lifestyle has always inspired me to create recipes that are "just as good" as the "real thing." She was an enormous inspiration—and willing taste-tester—for this book.

About the Author

Ramin Ganeshram is the author of seven cookbooks and two culinary novels. She is a food historian and trained chef who also contributes food articles to major publications. She lives in Connecticut with her family.

Index